BLACK TEETH

Black Teeth

& other North End Souvenirs

Ryszard Dubanski

Signature Editions

Cover design by Doowah Design.
Front cover photo of Ryszard Dubanski by F. Dubanski.
This book was printed on Ancient Forest Friendly paper.
Printed and bound in Canada by AGMV Marquis.

The following stories were previously published in slightly different versions: "Words of My Becoming" and "Cover All the Mirrors" in *Event*, and "Battlelines" in *subTerrain*.

We acknowledge the support of The Canada Council for the Arts and the Manitoba Arts Council for our publishing program.

Library and Archives Canada Cataloguing in Publication

Dubanski, Richard
Black teeth : and other North End souvenirs / Ryszard Dubanski.

ISBN 1-897109-02-4

1. Dubanski, Richard. 2. North End (Winnipeg, Man.). I. Title.

PS8607.U218B52 2005 C818'.603 C2005-904034-3

Signature Editions
P.O. Box 206, RPO Corydon, Winnipeg, Manitoba, R3M 3S7

for my brother Victor—
and for displaced persons everywhere

Contents

Black Teeth

The teacher told me to introduce myself to my grade one class at Margaret Scott Elementary. Not just me. We all had to do it, all the grade ones, on the first day of school. The teacher, grey-haired, patient though slightly twitchy Mrs. Williams, did it herself first, to show you how, telling us her name and where she lived, number and street. Then she looked at you silently and nodded, smiling firmly with her bright red lips, going down one row, up the next, and you stood up, came to the front of the room, turned around to face the class then said your name and your address.

Five or six kids had already done it when she looked at me. So I knew what to do.

I stood up, just like the others. And everything was fine, until I opened my mouth, that is. "Richard Dubanski," I said, in English, or as English as I could. In the front row, leaning by the window, Mrs. Williams breathed in, a kind of soft gasping sound. What had happened? There was a moment of deadening silence, and then my classmates started to whisper around me. I thought I heard "look," or maybe "yuck," wasn't sure. A few girls at the back of the room giggled.

I turned to Mrs. Williams. The teacher's face went worried for a moment, but then her reassuring red smile came right back. "That's fine, Richard," she said. I stood there, waiting for something, though not sure what. "Sit down," she said, before I had a chance to mention 992 Alfred Avenue.

Later, at recess, I kept to myself, wandering along the schoolyard fence until the bell went, calling us back to our fixed, box-like desks. I practised a vocabulary list in my head—"crazy, stupid, nuts"—trying not to hear pockets of mostly whispered talk about the weirdo, the "DP kid with the freak teeth." But no one actually spoke to me, so I kept at my silent word work. I had been sent to grade one with very few English words, and fewer still that I felt confident enough to say out loud. I knew "freak," and "teeth," though I had never before considered them together in this context, or as applying to me. The words, all the words spoken here at Margaret Scott, the name of my school, felt foreign, odd in my head or mouth. We had already been in Canada two years but my mother would not tolerate English at home, a way of preserving our Polish birthright, I guess. She seemed sure I would just pick it up, what I needed for school, on my own day to day. And actually, I could understand some things, more than I could say. I knew it was all up to me.

I don't know how the black teeth happened or when they came, exactly. Some kind of high fever, my mother said, that went on a couple of days. She made it sound ordinary and felt no need to inquire further, by calling a doctor, I mean. It was, after all, normal for young children to have fevers and nearly die in her Old World experience. Or die. That happened, too, often it seemed, from her stories and those of my relatives. Besides, doctors cost money, something we didn't have.

No doubt post-war DP camp life, from birth to age three in Sherwood Forest (*the* Sherwood Forest of merry men fame), didn't help build strong healthy teeth: my mother still spoke with bitterness of a meagre diet that allowed only a quart of milk and a couple of eggs per week, how they poached forbidden rabbits on the English squire's posted lands to bolster their protein portion, and so on. But they were only baby teeth, so what did it matter? It was nothing unusual, my mother said; I was getting to be a big boy and would grow out of them soon anyway. They still worked, as she said; that was the important thing. And I wasn't really concerned about them, or even that aware of my teeth, except when they felt a bit wobbly through raw vegetables, or meat, which I didn't like anyway.

At home after school that first day, I looked into the mirror. Mouth closed, I was a regular boy, just another six-year-old with dark brown hair, brown eyes shiny, white face. Open the mouth, though—

I did. My front teeth all along the top were burnt black, like lozenges of coal with corrugated edges, pointy, ugly, with spaces between that you could see through. All the top teeth you could see, the front eight. See this: white skin, brown hair and eyes, black line of charcoal splitting the face. Freak, weirdo, monster-boy.

Of course I'd stood in front of a mirror before, but I hadn't *looked* before, hadn't understood the purpose of the mirror, how it showed the true state of things in reversed order. I closed my lips, practised smiling and mouthing English words without baring my teeth. It could be done quite easily—if I had only known. But no one had told me, not my mother, not my father, not my few Polish-speaking occasional playmates, the sons and daughters of my parents' friends. This was something you had to find out for yourself.

At first I wanted to tell my mother what had happened at school, then decided against it; after all, my cinder teeth were normal at home. Why let her know that outside this house I was a freak, and she was the mother of one? Maybe I shouldn't trust her. Maybe, in Poland where people had oak furniture and made their own linen, every little kid had teeth like mine.

And, *really*, what was there to say? What had happened? In a way, nothing; in another, nothing that could be changed.

Carefully slow, I arrived at school next day with no time to spare, slipping into the lineup to enter our classroom without talking to anybody. In a single moment life had become complicated, cut off from its previous seamless unity. Now I existed in two worlds in which all things would be opposed, shifting between poles of meaning, mirror realms that imaged back their flip sides: black/white, normal/not-normal, good/bad.

I could manage. Best to slide by, without being noticed. I saw kids looking, smiling, pointing, laughing with their bright even white teeth, but again no one spoke to me directly. Then the bell rang and everyone proceeded orderly into the classroom, me buried among them, head down, just another normal kid heading for the desks. I walked in exactly like the others, matching perfectly, but Mrs. Williams saw me, stopped me at the classroom door: "Richard, the school nurse wants to see you."

My heart began to pound—singled out again, with everyone looking interested. I started to back away into the hall. "Wait," said Mrs. Williams.

I stopped. Something else wrong. What?

"Do you know where the nurse's office is?"

I shook my head.

"Down this hall, behind the big glass door—can you see it?" She pointed over my shoulder, almost but not quite touching me. I nodded. "O-K," she said slowly, putting a pause between the O and the K.

The nurse's office was green and white and smelled like soap. It had two chairs, a metal table, a sink and counter, and above, on the wall, a mirror which opened out. It was half open now, behind it there were shelves with glass bottles, pale wood sticks like from Popsicles, and boxes with red crosses. The nurse, pretty, all in white, short blonde hair under her cap, smiled, showing even wet white teeth like shiny sucked candies, all matched and lined up behind her pale pink lips. She said, "Are you Richard? Sit down here." She opened the mirror and took a Popsicle stick from the shelf. "Nothing to worry about. Open your mouth, please," she said. I opened it, pulling in my lips taut over my teeth. She touched my tongue with the stick, pulled back. "All righty—now smile."

I curved my closed lips upward, but already she knew. Mrs. Williams had told.

"Like this," the nurse said, smiling more, smiling crazily, so that her pink gums could be seen above her top teeth. "Like me. See, Richard?"

I tried to pull the corners of my mouth up further without showing my teeth.

"No, Richard, I need you to *smile* for me," the nurse said, still kindly.

I wanted to please her, but it was impossible; my worlds would collide, smash together, break like teeth. She put her fingers on my upper lip, gently. "I have to see...inside." We both waited, but nothing happened. Then she pushed on my upper lip, stared for a moment, took her hand away. "Okey-dokey," she said. "Do you know your home telephone number?"

"No telephone."

She looked at me, a long moment, then said: "Right, step out into the hall for a minute." I waited there until she came out with an envelope that she handed to me. "For your mother; do you understand? It's...important. Your mother needs to come here and see the principal tomorrow at 3:30. That's what the note says. Can you remember that? If there are problems...reading it...you can tell her. Or she can ask a, a neighbour, maybe?"

I pushed the envelope down inside my shirt and nodded hard, backing away to escape, then veered down the hall and returned to class. The principal, I thought, the principal. Anyone could tell this was a big trouble situation. The envelope crackled stiff inside my shirt, poked me as I sat down, trouble already.

Next day, we were in the office, the three of us. To everything the principal said, my mother kept answering "Only baby tooth," and "Not *tooth* tooth,"over and over.

Eventually the principal leaned forward across his desk, and raised his voice slightly. He frowned. I could see steel shining around his teeth, his tongue moving behind them. "Well, you see," he said, speaking very slowly, "it...this may be a dental con-di-tion...a health problem that requires...pro-fess-ional attention. Besides, we can't have children going around like..." He raised his left hand toward me, then dropped it.

My mother had stopped responding. She stood perfectly still, her face expressionless as bread, with me at her side, my mouth firmly shut.

"Do—you—have—a dentist?" he asked.

Nothing.

"Well, here." He scribbled on a notepad. "Here's the address of a good one...right around the corner on Selkirk." My mother took the note, stared at it, stuck it in her purse, said "Tank you," unsmiling, and we left together. On the way home she said nothing more.

Somehow it was arranged and a few days later, first thing in the morning, I was at the address, up in the big chair, blinking under the hard white light. I was scared, but also grateful: my teeth would now be fixed, I would look, be, just like every other kid in my class. I would be happy every day. The dentist, Dr. Finkleman, came in. He was gentle, kindly, with cool large hands that smelled like oranges. The chair swung back through the air. His fingers were suddenly in my mouth. "Just a few minutes now, take it easy," he said. "This won't hurt much. "

It hurt a lot. It took a long time. Afterwards the dentist said, "You are a brave boy. Nurse, wash Richard's face."

At home I went to bed and slept in the daytime, then woke up. When the bleeding stopped that evening, I went into the bathroom, turned on the light and leaned close to the mirror. I opened my mouth wide, looked in.

Now I had no teeth at all.

PLENTY

When I was seven, my route to school was carefully planned. Eastward on Alfred Avenue I'd walk, over the train tracks, around the corner, usually down Manitoba Street, sometimes down Burrows because it took me past the spire of St. John Cantius—after all, he was the patron saint of Poland, a great teacher, the Sunday school nuns said, who taught long ago for many years at also-famous Cracow University. Sometimes I'd go straight up Alfred to Arlington, where my school was, Margaret Scott Elementary, named after an energetic nurse who had worked hard to improve life for the working class immigrant enclave of the North End. I pictured someone pretty and blonde, like our school nurse, handing out...what? I wasn't sure, but something good and useful, maybe Mercurochrome?

By either route, I always made sure to pass the two corner grocery stores that lay between me and my destination. Originally modest little homes, they had been transformed by rectangular box-like additions to their fronts, one stuccoed and the other with faded wooden siding that matched the original house parts, both with big square windows. Unlike regular houses, they came right up to the sidewalk, pushed out onto the street, metamorphosed into that magical incarnation, the grocery-home.

Nowadays, corner stores have extras like fax machines or photocopiers. But their essence remains the same: foodstuffs up front and the families living in back; a TV or radio can usually be heard playing from somewhere in the living area. Often one of the family members will be sitting on a chair squarely placed between the two realms, one eye on the TV and the other on shelves of Campbell's soups, Heinz ketchup, Kraft Dinner, Ritz crackers, Libby's Fruit Cocktail, canned pork n' beans, various candies and chocolate bars, cigarettes up high beyond the front counter—back then, mostly Players, Matinées, Export A—a cooler holding bottles of milk and tubs of ice cream, and so on.

In those earlier days, the grocery-home fascinated me. It was all I could possibly want, an absolute refutation to my mother's stories of never enough: starvation in Siberia, fights for a potato during the war, hunger rations in the DP camp. Here there were shelves and shelves of glittering canned goods, candies, drinks—everything, unlike the limited and sometimes barren larder at our little *chandah* (shack) by the tracks. When you stepped inside a grocery-home, often there was no one even there, in the store part, I mean, no one guarding the hoard, and for a moment you'd be alone in this treasure trove of goodies, transfixed by plenty like some Aladdin stumbling into a genie's cave of wonders. Then the father, mother, or son/daughter schoolkid clerking between bouts of homework came in, to see who was there and to ring up your order. Tantalizing smells drifted from the darkened domesticity beyond, where the rest of the family stayed, inside the home part, having supper maybe, or lunch, a cup of coffee or tea.

Often I entered not to buy anything, because I didn't have any money, but on a personal reconnaissance mission, researching all the different grocery-homes in the neighbourhood, not just the two on the route to school. Each was a little different, and I just liked to meditate on the cans of soup, tins of salmon, boxes of Corn Flakes, cookies with names I didn't understand (Oreo?), the oddly shaped corned beef cans from Argentina. To dream…

But it was a perilous business, my obsession. The grocery-homers looked at me strangely. Some would ask rudely what I wanted, then send me sharply on my way. And one day a huge Great Dane jumped unexpectedly out a grocery-home's tiny fenced yard and attacked me. It leapt up, yowling in a deep-throated basso profundo, then stopped. For a moment we stood eye to shiny brown eye. It scrutinized my face uncertainly, and then clamped its huge salivating black mouth on my left wrist. A token bite, not really serious, didn't break the skin. Still, I was terrified, and remained afraid of dogs for many years after.

Another day, I came across a stack of newspapers on the corner of the street where one of the grocery-homes stood. The bundle was just sitting there, maybe fifty copies, obviously having fallen from the sky, or been lost by someone. I stooped to contemplate this gift, not knowing what to make of it. Finally I twisted a few copies of the *Winnipeg Free Press* out of the pile, then started for home, unsure about what to do with the newspapers since neither of my parents read English and I didn't read, period—when an angry grey-faced man in a flannel robe and slippers rushed out of his grocery-home and yelled at me. I dropped the papers and ran. It was years later I realized that was how papers were delivered to corner stores, just dumped on the street or sidewalk in front of them.

Despite these close calls, at bedtime I still prayed my family might one day own one of those miraculous grocery-homes, where we would all live happily. In the morning, when I woke up, I'd stay in bed for a minute or two, eyes shut, imagining what it would be like to wake up in a grocery-home instead.

Everything would be so different: in my pyjamas, I'd pad downstairs while the household slept, turn on all the lights in the store part, go out among our laden shelves before we were open for business, wander up and down, and then reach up and grab: anything I wanted, anything I felt like. No shortages, always a surplus—that was true freedom and meant never having to worry again.

Battle Lines

It was 1959, and I knew we were at war. We lived in a tiny two-room house, a flat-roofed box fronted by two towering linden trees, a few doors down from the dead end at the railway tracks. That was our first home in Winnipeg, on Alfred Avenue. I was ten.

I started to notice that the streets around our house, our block, all had military names—Artillery, Battery, Burrows, Sgt. Tommy Prince. But in a deeper way it seemed I had always known. Even the Alfred immortalized in our address was martial, a warrior English king discussed in history class at school. It all fit, war words to commemorate armaments, battle tactics, and soldiers. World War II had taken my parents, a corporal and a military nurse, from Poland to Siberia, then down through the Mideast and across Europe. They were demobbed in England, in a DP camp where they got over their

TB symptoms enough to migrate to Canada. So the stories I heard at home were full of war words, too: "battalion," "Monte Casino," "casualties," "artillery."

Old and new conflicts were being discussed all the time in after-dinner talks between my parents and their war-surviving comrades: Poles, plus some Ukrainians, a Russian or two. Prideful, involuntary émigrés, they frequently argued, fell out and stopped speaking over issues like The "Nukular" Race. Radio news was full of how the Post-War had become the Cold War, and although no one seemed exactly sure what that meant, we were constantly reminded of its threat.

Trains were also important, a crucial part of the overall War Machine—and there we were, right next to the railway tracks. That's how soldiers were transported to the front lines, in boxcars, trains roaring through the night to a distant map-point for deadly action at dawn. Often I'd wake in the night to the keening of a train whistle, the close throb of its passing, and think about war.

Then there was Her Majesty, the Queen. Four years before, back in grade one at Margaret Scott Elementary, one day there was a big ceremony to mark the coronation of Elizabeth II. We all stood in lines in the auditorium, like a company of soldiers, gazing up at the teachers on stage with the principal and several other important officials, listening to the new queen make her address over the radio in delicate, halting tones. I didn't understand the speech, but kept hearing words like "freedom" and "democracy," important fighting words that even at age six I recognized.

We sang "God Save the Queen," and were each given a commemorative coin. It had the royal profile on one side, over the ER insignia, something ancient looking on the other. It lay heavy in my hand, heavy as a silver dollar but a dark, burnished brown. I took it home, kept it safe, hidden.

I knew the war was over, had seen it finish again and again in newsreels and war movies at the Selkirk Avenue cinema where I'd go with my mother Saturday nights when she was too restless to sit in her tiny featureless house. But things were mixed up; I also knew the war was still going on, in a secret way. Signs were all around, for those who could interpret them. Trains, street names, war stories, the Empire—as I grew older, seven, eight, I could see that it all added up. I became watchful and silent, like a spy, keeping my secret knowledge of the ongoing war to myself. Talking could be dangerous.

The final proof, if more were needed, was the continuing food shortage. Year after year, there was never quite enough to go around the table; clearly supplies were running low...possibly being blockaded by the enemy. According to Mother, the cupboard was often bare, except for home-grown potatoes; boiled, mashed, baked, roasted, fried, and grated, they were our staple food, appearing in pancakes, soups, salads, pyrogies, *piluski* ("little fingers") at breakfast, lunch, and dinner.

The world was confused and dangerous, which is why I needed a gun. All I had was a silly piece of plywood shaped roughly like a rifle. I needed *real* protection; yet I wasn't exactly scared. In fact, most of the time I was pretty happy. I just wanted to be a good little soldier, to do my duty.

My father would not talk about war things with me (he didn't talk much anyway), but I'd seen how real guns worked: on the *Roy Rogers Show* at Rosie's place, on TV, a rarity those days. Their set was brand new, only the second one on the block. We were in grade three together, and she asked me over, coveted invitation, to watch one Saturday afternoon. I saw how guns quickly cleared things up, especially confusion. Bang, bang—Roy would shoot his silver guns—and everything went back to normal, with Dale smiling sweetly, Trigger snorting, and Roy grinning.

At once and more than anything I wanted a pair of ivory-handled silver six-shooters, with studded leather holsters, like Roy's. I *needed* them. At home I grew pale, ran a fever, and had to be put to bed sick. Trigger I could live without, but I made my mother promise at the shadowy bedside that as soon as we had enough money, she would buy the guns for me.

Rosie lived two doors down in a small bungalow, with her parents, a younger sister, and Grandma. Maybe Rosie felt sorry for me, the poor Polack kid who wore shorts and suspenders, had prison-camp haircuts done by his dad, and didn't know English "so good." Or it could have been something else. She didn't have many girl buddies, didn't do girl things with dolls and such. Maybe we were both a little weird, not quite fitting in, and that's why we began to hang out more and more, playing games, watching her parents' TV when they got one, and, from the start of our relationship to when I became ten, exploring the ditches.

Ditches were my specialty, important for many reasons. Fortunately they were close by; the train tracks, only a few metres from our doors, were flanked on both sides by ditches, scooped-out lozenge shapes, each a block long between the avenues. Now they're gone, filled in. You just see broad flat swathes of grass on either side of the track. Back then they were alpine valleys, a vast military network of trenches (in which my buddies and I killed each other with our wooden weapons), or, in a different season, a string of blue-green lakes reaching the horizon. Before I knew Rosie, someone told me the tracks ran to Winnipeg Beach and beyond, way up north; but that meant nothing to me—I had never been there, and didn't care. The ditches demarcated my world, the whole of it, from one end of the year to the other.

Ditches were connected to war and, therefore, to the war that I knew was going on in deadly secret at the edges of my life. Soldiers often died in ditches, "trench warfare" it was called—I'd seen it in movies—shot and bleeding, blown up by cannon fire or riddled with machine gun bullets, drowned in summer in a foot or two of bloody water or frozen over in winter as the cold sun set in the snow-blind West.

These were some of the things I taught Rosie over the years. Even at eleven, a year older than me, she knew little about war. And she was also a girl, yes, but that didn't matter. I had other buddies, boys, and that was fine. With Rosie it was also fine yet at the same time completely different. She never lied or told crazy stories the way guys did, always trying to top each other. Rosie was not like them; she never fibbed or exaggerated, and, though lying was fun, I liked that about her. Always, Rosie was serious, choosing her words carefully, thinking, frowning over problems—I trusted her completely even though she was a girl.

In winter the ditches filled with snow. Crossing them was forbidden, because every spring, when the melt came, bodies of dead snow-drowned children were recovered from their depths. But Rosie and I played chicken on them, in the late afternoons when the sun was setting and it was almost time to go in for the long prairie night, daring each other to walk on the crisp sparkling crust that bridged who knew how deep a cache of snow. Sometimes you crossed safely—sometimes you crashed through. Both sensations were eerie, nauseous, thrilling. When I broke through the top layer, I'd fall swift as a dream to the hips or even, one time, the armpits, held fast in a numbing shaft of unyielding white like a trapped soldier, until Rosie pushed her toboggan up to my frost-burned face so I could grab on and crawl out.

Then, as winter turned to spring, the snow would finally vanish, sometimes as late as May. The ditches filled with meltwater, and were transformed into giant inland seas to be navigated and charted, each at first glance like the next, but in reality quite different, depending on what the gleaming surface concealed.

With water came life: flourishing in tall grasses—with special English names like "thistles," "blue flag," "bulrushes"; then there were mosquitoes, a million shiny slimy bugs crawling on the rock slope near the tracks, worms and even small snakes ess-ing their ways along the lake edges, tadpoles flitting beneath (soon to be spotted frogs: I'd seen the stages, the arm buds bulging), spiders dancing gravity-defying jigs on the transparent skin of water, and dragonflies, skimming the shimmering surface in mechanical precision, like tiny helicopters, an abrupt dazzle of green or blue in the ozonized air. Rosie liked the big golden dragonflies best, especially when they flew up to your face, brilliant with sun, close in with a faint buzz, and you could see the pattern of alien life in their iridescent eyes. She would go dead still then, like a magic statue of a girl, willing them to land—and sometimes they would.

The ditches were used as garbage dumps year-round, and the "lakes" formed by the spring melt usually derived their names from what they held, besides life. So there was no Dragonfly Lake. People threw in all sorts of trash from passing train windows, or furtively came by to toss stuff in when no one was looking at night. Car tires, doorknobs, toasters, burnt-out pots and kettles, busted radios, bike parts, vacuums, bedsprings, boxes, broken toys. You'd be scouting, then spot something on the bottom, out in the deep yet clear middle of the lake—a car bumper, maybe, its wet chrome catching shivery circlets of light. That's when you'd start telling your friends to meet you at Bumper Lake.

In late spring the lakes were at their fullest and most alluring. After the dead emptiness of long winter months, the busy life they contained was fantastical and seductive, distracting me from my soldier's purpose, my watchfulness. Underwater life seemed defiantly undefined, like anything could happen and be equally OK. Constant shape-shifting from one kind to another seemed the only rule, an endless play of possibilities, first plant, then insect, then animal life—the lakes became my personal magic show, a Wide World of Life kit...just add water.

As the short, blistering prairie summer took hold, the lakes would evaporate and—inch by inch—disappear. When the waters were gone, I showed Rosie how the lake bottoms yielded up their secrets, and we scoured for treasure on dry land.

In high summer we spent whole days in the dried-out ditches, setting them up as trenches, or playing Hide and Seek, Rosie's favourite, seeking out the best places to camouflage ourselves. She'd scream in apparent terror when discovered, but never actually ran away; there'd be a pause, then it would be my turn to hide. You could reconnoitre endlessly in among the tall ditch grasses and never be spied from street level.

When evening came we watched the train return from the north, sailing by in metal majesty, sunburnt day-trippers waving at us from its sliding windows. Sometimes we put coins on the tracks to get flattened. Of course we had no watches, no train schedules to follow. Instead we listened to the rails, heads down and ears pressed to the steel, waiting for the unmistakable watery hum trains made as they approached invisibly from miles away. Then we'd put down a penny, to retrieve it after the train passed, thin as paper now, the diameter of a silver dollar, unrecognizably blank. I wanted to try a silver dollar, which I'd heard would spread like a dinner plate; but how could anyone afford it? Once I considered the Queen's commemorative coin, but it was too important, too noble for experimentation.

As if to test my warrior's mettle, one golden August afternoon while digging in my parents' garden, under orders to turn sod for upcoming potato plantings, my shovel hit something hard. Clunk, a dull metallic sound. I sank the shovel again, brought up a mud-clogged thing roughly the size of a pie plate, and turned it over on the worm-glistening earth.

I dropped the shovel and picked up the mysterious object. It was strangely heavy. I started clearing away the muck, and in a moment saw the shape of a gun emerging: a long, slender barrel followed by a contoured back-angled handle with some bumps at the top. It had a weird futuristic look. I kept cleaning away the mud until I could stick my finger into the trigger hole; the pistol was so awkward and heavy I needed both hands to keep it upright.

"Look what *I* found, Rosie!" We met at Suitcase Lake, long dried up. I had cleaned and polished the gun, even rubbed a bit of 3-in-1 Oil into the dulled metal, and hidden it a few days before, wrapped in rag, under a big rock. Now I lifted it in both hands and held it toward her.

Rosie crinkled up her eyes, squinting through light brown lashes at me, and looked at the gun for a long moment. A kind of shiver passed over her face. "That's a 'Luger,'" she said. "I saw one on TV, spies use 'em. What...what're you going to do with it?"

Rosie looked scared, her thin shoulders hunching up, hands clutched behind her back. I'd wanted to surprise her, and was pleased by the effect my find was having—but that was a good question. What could I *do* with a Luger, at least until I grew strong and big enough to hold it in one hand like a good soldier?

"Is it...loaded?" she asked.

"Nah," I lied. I hadn't actually checked, not knowing how to with an automatic that wasn't like a Roy Rogers pistol, where all you had to do was twirl the chamber.

I put the gun back in its hiding place, made Rosie swear she'd tell no one; I needed time to think. This was serious, the secret war had reached out and touched me directly. A Luger buried in our backyard. Maybe the spies knew I knew—maybe they would come back for it one night. I had to be on guard. But how? Against who?

With no good plan, I just left the gun hidden there, half-forgetting it. At the same time, I dreamt of guns night after night: having one would change my life, make me a hero, lead to some dramatic action in which I defended the Empire, maybe saved her young Majesty. But most of my dreams featured lovely silver six-shooters, not the ugly, black, clunky Luger, which I left in the ditch, checking on it at intervals through the fall and into winter.

One afternoon in November, just after Rosie's eleventh birthday, on a quiet Sunday the first snowfall came. She and I were in the former Lawnmower Lake. About a foot of wet, heavy snow lay on the ground. We were playing our own private version of Duel, the prime rule being that whoever dodged, ducked, or moved in any way, lost a round.

We stood firmly in our spots, legs apart, like cowboys ready to shoot it out, about twenty-five feet from each other. Though Rosie was a bit taller, we were fairly well matched; the results of our duels running at around fifty/fifty.

It wasn't dangerous, armoured as we were by quilted parkas with fake-fur-lined hoods, thick scarves covering chins, and boots laced to the knees. We scooped up snow, packed our balls, and took turns throwing.

Rosie was wearing a white parka, pale yellow scarf, matching mitts, and white boots. "Here it comes," she cried, lobbing a big one. She laughed as it caught me on the arm, above the elbow, with a solid thump.

"Didn't feel a thing," I lied; it had stung. I put the finishing touches on a small, densely packed ball. Rosie made a difficult target in the snow, mostly in white and against the sun. I whipped it at her but without much hope of a hit, thinking it was time to suggest changing sides. That would be fairer—maybe with the sun behind me I'd have a better chance.

The snowball disappeared into the pale glaring sky—when I heard it connect with a splat I was surprised, pleased by my good luck. Then I saw where the snowball had caught her, just above the scarf round her neck, at the side of her face.

For a moment the world was silent. Rosie stood there, a white-on-white figure in the ditch, the houses and bare trees beyond flattened to insignificance by the blank winter light.

As I stared, a spot of red in the middle blotted out everything: a dot of blood on Rosie's cheek. Like I had shot her. She touched the spot, saw the blood, pulled off her scarf, burst into tears, and ran.

I ran after her: "Rosie, sorry—I didn't mean…"

She didn't listen, just headed for her house and slammed the gate behind her, sobbing and stumbling through the front door without a backward glance. A piece of ice or something, I guessed, got stuck in my snowball. I waited for a while at the gate, then went home.

Next afternoon Rosie's grandma came over and told my mother how I had, without provocation and in a vicious sneak attack, wounded their Rosie to the point of drawing blood, treacherously striking her in the face with an "illegal" iceball. I was kept in the house for a week, and gained the nickname "Girl Killer" in the neighbourhood.

Christmas came and my aunt from St. Louis arrived for a visit; she brought with her a boxed set of Roy Rogers cap guns, plus a matching white cowboy hat. I was no longer punished. Right after that I told Raymond, the weird twenty-year-old guy who kept hanging round us kids all the time, about the Luger, and agreed to sell it to him. He gave me five bucks, stuffed the gun into a green Army surplus duffle bag, and took off. I didn't see him over the rest of the winter, and in spring heard that he had left town.

After New Year, Rosie and I started playing again, but things weren't the same. She never admitted she'd lied about what had really happened. After the first time we talked, it was never mentioned; she was obdurate, opaque, sly.

"If you really think I did it on purpose, why are you playing with me?" I asked her.

There was no answer, she just stared at me. It was as if the rules had suddenly been altered without me being told, and we were no longer on the same side. Rosie seemed different after that; she would giggle for no reason and sometimes wore dresses. One day when we met at Suitcase Lake it looked like she had lipstick on.

That's when I started to hang out more with the guys. They respected me as the Girl Killer. At home, I polished my Roy Rogers six-guns and practised fast-drawing them in front of the mirror. I was full of regret and yearning, dreaming of one day having the real thing.

SIRENS

The city's air-raid siren wailed in the early morning air. Assaulting, confusing, alarming, its tone was constant yet seemed to rise steadily to some fatal extreme. So this was it, I thought, the actual End.

There was no panic. We'd seen the filmstrips and read the "In the event of..." handouts, so we knew what to do. We'd actually done it twice already, though never so early in the day. As one, the class stood up, leaving our post-Communion breakfast untouched on the scarred old desktops. On command we turned to the back of the room, paused, filed out.

The emergency exit at the end of the top of the third floor landing was our goal: a dark, closed-in metal chute that hugged the side of the building, spiraling down to the ground far below. Its hatch-like door reminded me of submarines—now I was the guy from the war flick, grim-faced, a hero stepping through the dark hatch, then abruptly dead in close-up at the bottom of the sea, blood feathering up pink from one ear. Dead: my stomach closed like a fist as I thought the word. Yes, I would be dead, atomized into radiant rags of flesh. Would I even survive to feel burning, to scream? Would I still have a mouth? We would all be dead, right in this steel tube, slipping down, our mixed bodies torn and fragmented like fresh sausage getting pressed into casings at Jankowski's Meats on Main Street.

My heart thumped and leapt at the pictures I saw, yet on I went right through the black opening, just as Pete and the Fat Girl, Danuta, or Doughnut, as we sometimes called her, had gone before me, calmly, like robots. Just as Pete and the Fat Girl had done, I sat down feet-first on the cool grey metal of the slide, and began to fall.

Round and round and down we went—forty-seven bums from Sister Caroline's grade six class buffing the chute to a silver sheen that late September 1962 morning, in North End Winnipeg. Whoosh, steel-smelling breeze touching my face, the siren's shriek a strange metal music, my legs the perfect 90- degree angle to chase Danuta's bulky red-sweatered shape fleeing before me. At once my mood shifted. I laughed—Doomsday was fun, a wild toboggan ride. I might never write another exam, never have to answer another question; I could do what I liked, as long as I died quite soon.

Technique was important—by leaning deep into the spiral I gained speed, my loafers eagerly nudging Danuta's rear at the narrowest point of each turning curve, a dizzy, throbbing rhythm of contact and disjunct. At last we popped out, still alive, first her, then me, out of the open hatch at ground level to throw ourselves at once against the brick building with the rest of our school population. "Cling on for dear life" was how we'd been instructed for this final step by the nuns—this was the drill, first down the escape chute, then fast against the side of the building, to shield ourselves from the deadly A-bomb rays. That was how you survived.

You had to be cool about it, of course. And we were, totally cool. No one was scared, for Chrissake, by an air-raid siren or a nuclear war exercise; no one in our grade six class was afraid of fire, pestilence, death, Judgement Day, or the End of the World.

Sister Augustine, our stern and usually sad-faced principal, sailed past me to claim a spot further down the wall. Like me, she looked skyward—but, it crossed my mind, she was probably seeking something like the Four Horsemen of the Apocalypse rather than airplanes. Her eyes were oddly bright—her normally sallow cheeks glowed. The End of Planet Earth would not be a bad thing to her; she might even be praying for it, I suddenly realized. Heavenly Choirs, Salvation, Rapture, and Eternal Bliss, all just a moment of fission away.

The siren kept on wailing. I shivered and looked around, checking to see where my guys were: Pete, Rick, Larry, Stan, John. Nowhere in sight. I was about to slip around the back of the school to join them for a smoke, when another nun, beautiful Sister Lioba, spotted my move. "Cling on!" she commanded in her sweet history class voice.

So I was caught. You couldn't really cling, but I pressed back into the wall, observing its rectangular grid, my palms receiving its sharp brick edges and rough, gritty imprint. Next to me was the Fat Girl, round faced, with the same curly brown hair and goofy smile I'd known since grade four, and next to her, kitty-corner against the built-in pillar was Faye, the weirdly beautiful girl from Flin Flon, a quiet and shy Métis who boarded in the Benedictine convent across the street where the nuns lived. Her big moist eyes glowed like back-lit amber; her straight black hair hung almost to her waist. The three of us were boxed in on the far side of the chute where there wasn't much room for others, cut off for the moment from visual monitoring by our peers.

"We're all going to die," Faye offered me in her delicately accented English, showing bright white teeth, the left front one slightly chipped at the bottom.

Except for the Fat Girl, girls didn't talk much to boys outside of class, not just to exchange a casual observation like this; the nuns did not encourage mixing. Things were out of sync, for sure; that wasn't surprising, considering that once again the End of the World might be upon us. I looked over at the Fat Girl, checking her reaction to Faye's unexpected boldness. The Fat Girl grinned, her familiar big crazy grin; but for once she chose to stay quiet.

"Don't sweat it," I told Faye, "Early Warnin's just doin' its job." I shrugged, then looked up; secretly I was straining to hear Russki planes above the siren's scream, that special whine of an A-bomb you heard in the newsreels, with *our* name on it—Holy Ghost Parochial—the one that would "nuke" us (interesting new word) to less than smithereens, send *us* Heavenward...at least, those of us who'd done our First Friday thing this morning.

It was the same on the first Friday of every month; the whole school went to mass so that we could take the sacrament of Holy Communion. All Catholic schools did it that way round the world, multitudes redeemed, millions and millions of kids swallowing the little cotton-tasting hosts at more or less the same moment. The whole day was, in fact, semi-special. First, you had to fast from midnight (not such a big deal as you were probably asleep). Then, in the morning, you had to brush your teeth without swallowing *anything*—one single drop of water oozing past your tonsils would bar you from eating the Body and drinking the Blood. Not to mention potentially doom you, if, just for example, you happened to get caught in an atomic bomb blast while in a state of sin. That would be tough luck, bad timing.

And because of all this—the crucial importance of fasting, yet breakfast being the most important meal of the day—after Communion we actually ate at school, in our classrooms, on these significant Fridays. This break from routine was cool: eating at a desk you normally did Latin on, being *allowed and even encouraged* to have your mouth full in class (normally a punishable and frequently punished offense), all this was subversive, pleasurable, sweet; it suggested that life could change, rules could shift. Like an A-bomb wiping out school, church, and hometown in one great shining whack, everything could be altered. Though, of course, alteration here was less sweeping, and was itself surrounded by its own rules—you *had* to order your First Friday breakfast the Friday before, the last one of the previous month, and your choices were only lemon *or* cherry Danish, chocolate *or* plain milk. But still it was violation, therefore exciting...besides, you could have as much as you could pay for.

Sometimes I'd be sent down to the street with one or two others to help bring up the Danishes from the bakery truck. They arrived in big flat white pastry boxes, one colour—egg-yolk yellow or translucent red—per box, fragrant, sugar-flecked shining gold crisp around the bright centres, all covered loosely with wax paper. Delicious. We were just about to start our belated, pious breakfasting when the siren sounded this morning.

As if tuned in to my thoughts, Danuta spoke up. Her voice was hesitant, harsh, straining maybe to be heard over the endless call of the siren: "Too...too bad they had to pick First Friday, and right after Communion."

I knew just what she meant, I thought—I was hungry, too. "Yeah," I said, "I could use a Danish for sure." Quickly I searched the sky through narrowed eyes for responding B-52s streaking from bases deep in the Dakotas, then looked back at her.

Danuta, to my surprise, was giving me an irritated, wide-eyed look, as if I'd said something absolutely, incredibly stupid. Faye, on the other hand, smiled. Maybe she liked me now, thought I was *really* cool, fearless, my guy appetite unaffected by the still-shrieking siren, the threat of imminent death; though actually it was a pure regret I'd voiced, not bravado...I was sad that I'd put myself down for only one Danish and the cheaper plain milk on what might be the actual last day of my life.

Faye fingered the silver cross at her throat. "At least *we're* saved," she said, looking toward the Fat Girl. "...if it really is the Nukular Bomb, this time. 'Cept if—"

She broke off as the siren wailed, the loudest yet, then resumed: "—if you're...*not* saved." Her thin fingers released the little crucifix—it flopped against her brown skin once, then lay still.

The Fat Girl looked at Faye for a moment, then spoke flatly. "Right. You're saved unless you're not saved."

Faye smiled. "If you're not *baptized*, or if you don't take *Communion*, or go to church, you know, like your *mom*, Doughnut; if you're not *Catholic*, like Rebecca Goldberg, or some *Mennonite*, then..."

Faye shrugged—the Fat Girl said nothing. Weird to see her not grinning, not laughing, not talking. Everyone knew she was a motor-mouth who could never keep quiet. Faint spots of colour had come into her cheeks from the cool morning air, but her face remained otherwise, uncharacteristically, blank. The girls looked at each other. Then both turned to stare at me, Faye still smiling, the Fat Girl more serious.

I looked away, thought about pale, black-eyed Rebecca; there were always one or two like that in school, non-Catholics who got a free period on these First Fridays. That wasn't fair—but at least they were going to Hell, whereas I was on my way either to Heaven or back to my cherry Danish. Unless Rebecca converted as the A-bomb fell. Religion was interesting that way: you could be a goodie-two-shoes 99.9% of the time, but one little mistake and you were damned to eternal flames. Or you could be a real scumbag all your life, or believe nothing, or the wrong thing, then repent on your deathbed and waltz straight through the Pearly Gates. Nothing was fair—that's the way God wanted it.

Faye and Danuta were still looking at me, like they were waiting for me to say something. So I said: "Should'a got a *chocolate* milk this time, and *two* cherry Danish." Nothing. They continued to stare like aliens using mind-meld power to create a forcefield. I floundered on, explaining. "If yer gonna get *nuked*, like, to death, I mean, might as well..." Silence. I looked back and forth between them, seeking a way out—but out of what? My eyes locked onto the Fat Girl's stony green-grey gaze. I had known her forever; but she seemed a stranger. "Fill 'er up—right, Doughnut?" I blurted, finally.

Faye answered for her, like they were best friends. "Oh, *Danuta* likes the *lemon* ones; they're her *favourites*."

Now for some reason the Fat Girl got madder—she widened her eyes and glared, not at Faye, but at me. Why? Meanwhile, Faye giggled, then stopped and began to twirl a piece of her long black hair, leaning her head to one side, swaying it back and forth. Her shoulder bumped against mine, then swayed away.

The siren went on; by now it felt as if the sound was inside my head, a part of me like an earache or a bruise. Danuta's eyes—strangely pale, a cloudy green that seemed slightly unnatural—were still fixed coldly on me. I had never noticed them before, thought they were brown. It was only later that I realized that they seemed to change colour, as if to match her changing moods, though this really did not make sense.

"*What?*" I said to her, staring back, thinking "The *Doughnut* likes *Danish*" over and over.

"What?" she replied.

"*What*, like, you know, is your prob—"

"I don't *have* a problem," she broke in. Then she turned to Faye. "Look, what are you trying to—"

Faye broke in, looking down. "I didn't say *anything*, just—"

The siren stopped, and there was a weird, deadened silence, as if something, though not an A-bomb, had dropped on us. We stood there frozen in time.

Now Faye spoke up again, but only to the Fat Girl. "*We* should go," she said, rotating her entire body away from me, making a girls-only contract with Danuta. "*We* will be in trouble." She began to walk quickly away to where the other students, little sucks, were already clustering at the side entry door, apparently dying to get back to class.

The Fat Girl followed her, but more slowly. As she passed me she said, "What I meant wasn't—I meant, too *bad*—we could'a gone to Hell, Ricky. You *know*?"

She smiled, paused for a moment; I saw her with the weak October sun behind her, bouncing off her hair, showing strands of red and gold. Up close, she didn't look all that fat. Then she, too, was gone, back with the others.

A voice called to me, not too loud, "Hey, Richard," and I turned to see one of my buddies, short and sturdy little blond Stan, coming toward me from the back of the building. Silently I watched his approach, raising my hand an inch in minimal greeting. He leaned back against the wall beside me, looked straight ahead.

"We grabbed a smoke, eh?" he said, and then, "What *happened* to you?"

"Got nuked," I told him. I pointed at an empty brown paper lunchbag, blowing agape across the school yard. "That's my fuckin' spleen, man. I'm toast."

We watched the bag together for a moment, in silence. I could smell the cigarette smoke on Stan, and felt regret. He opened his mouth, made like blowing a smoke ring at the sky, closed it. Then, slowly, we walked back toward the still open doors.

I was all worked up, really bugged. All this because of some crisis over missiles in Cuba, shiny weapons far away, a struggle for power. We lined up to go back into school, and I closed my eyes, seeing again the anger on Danuta's face, the brightness in her hair, Faye's hand touching the metal cross at her brown throat as she laughed. Faye's shoulder, warm, bumping me. The whole thing was stupid. What was Cuba to me? Some stupid little island in the Caribbean where everyone smoked cigars. Who cared?

THE BARBER OF SIBERIA

It was definitely not a scene from *The Barber of Seville*. There was nothing playful, and certainly nothing passionate or operatic about those haircut Saturday afternoons, stuck in our tiny beige kitchen, sitting on the blue vinyl stepstool between the stove and the table, a flour-sack tea-towel round my neck, and my always-silent father, lips pursed in concentration as he clipped my never-allowed-to-be long, dark, lank hair into a precise army style brush cut.

When I was very young I would be perched high on a stack of telephone books while my father wielded his big heavy clippers with the dull brass fittings, the actual pair that he used in his unit of the Polish Free Army in Egypt back in 1944. My mother had told me this, and it lent a slight aura of excitement to those early cuts, like the cool metal touching my head was almost a kind of gun. Barbering, according to my mother, had become part of my dad's soldierly duty—along with killing our enemies—when his unit was being trained by the British; that was when my dad became the official barber for the group, and I suppose it was when he received his official army barbering kit.

You don't think much about soldiers getting haircuts, but of course they do. Soldiers all used to have brush cuts, I guess, though it wasn't as if they could go into town weekly to keep their hair short; that would just be crazy. Besides, my father had already been the designated haircutter—using ordinary scissors—for his comrades in the Siberian slave labour camp where they had all first met the year before. Those were the stories, all courtesy of my mother, and there it was: mysterious, a kind of tonsorial destiny.

Snip, snip. In the early years, the historic clippers in his clenched right hand were quiet, they opened and closed rhythmically, almost gently, their two meshed blades crossing as he squeezed the handles, then springily released them.

Did he like doing it? Did he think about war and killing as he traveled over and around his son's head, making it like a soldier's? This process, on haircut days, was the only time he touched me. I liked it in a way, that fleeting physical contact as he ran his hand knowledgeably over my brow, moved my ear aside for the clippers, though I was already starting to hate forced haircuts, being stopped from playing, trapped like a prisoner, with no freedom to decide. Then, later, when I was around twelve, in the early sixties, he got modern electric clippers that moved fast and buzzed loudly next to your ear, like a menacing bee. The war clippers were put away, the process was speeded up, but the dreaded outcome, the army style buzz cut, remained the same.

My dad's former camp and army buddies, Canadian Pacific Railway workers now, came along on those Saturday afternoons to get their monthly cuts. For them it must have been a way to keep in contact, talk over the war days and their adventures, and to save some money too, even though they were all employed and did not have to worry so much about that side of things. So for them maybe it was enjoyable in that boring talky adult way. And it might even have been OK for me, if my dad had included me in the men's afternoon, the special atmosphere those days had; but he didn't, he always did me first, as if to be rid of me before his friends arrived. My mother usually disappeared on those afternoons, went shopping with her big brown alligator purse. When the old friends came, there was conversation—mostly Polish with bits of Ukrainian thrown in, gradually getting louder—and drinks as the pile of hair on the floor grew, my dark brown buried under blond, black, and increasingly, as years went by, iron grey. The men drank beer in the summertime, in the winter, all-purpose *wodka*, clear or flavoured with fruit like blackberries or blueberries. Sometimes, if I hung around without being noticed, I would even hear my normally laconic father come up with a few terse jokes. But not with me—with me my father never said much at all. Mostly he was silent, getting done with me, doing a no-nonsense job of it. Buzz, buzz.

More and more I hated the stupid weirdness of home barbering. Why me? Well, my little brother, eight years younger than me, was also getting the treatment. But every single kid my age I knew went to a barbershop for a normal, Canadian haircut. As my mother pointed out with her strange satisfaction, we were different, we didn't have cash for frivolities like "man's hair styling"—her lip curled as she said it. And she often mentioned, over our budget-minded dinners of homegrown cabbage, potatoes, and cheap Mennonite chicken, our non-unionized father made far less than his Canadian Pacific Railway pals, with their full "gravy-train" wage and benefit packages. Thrift was important and virtuous.

This did not make me like home haircuts any better. Nor did the fact that my father did a pretty decent job of his barbering. Sure, he was careful, gentle, and methodical—he was also doctrinaire in his absolute belief that all men looked and *felt* better with neat short hair. There was no question, no discussion about when or if I would get my next "trim." Every month was the rule, and it killed me that I would never look right, never be able to get a cool "duck's ass" or a Beatle cut. Thanks to my father I would never be normal and no girls would like me.

That's when I started stalking barbershops. They looked so jolly, in a manly way, the old-fashioned ones, I mean, before there were genderless modern salons. The barbershops I surveyed always sported traditional red, blue, and white poles, swirling in such a carefree manner that you couldn't tell up from down. Through their front windows you could see happy customers relaxing in big comfortable chairs while they got the exact haircut they wanted, often reading the paper, smoking cigars, utterly at ease. Ditto the friendly barber in his quieter, non-haircutting moments. The shops always looked welcoming, brightly lit, clean, cheerful.

The one I liked best was up towards St. John's High School. It was on a corner, an angled entry that welcomed customers from both streets equally, and inside a small cozy place, with just one leather chair, a coat rack, and what appeared to be an especially genial barber. I'd see him chatting amiably while he clipped, or sitting there on his own when not cutting, always smiling, reading the paper, smoking his pipe, as if he were perfectly content with customers or alone. You could just tell that he was a great guy, a regular guy.

All my life, even now, I've had this minor fascination with barbershops, at the same time a problem with barbers, a sort of attraction/repulsion feeling. It's a pretty intimate thing, after all, getting your hair cut, having someone you don't really know touch you, a stranger hovering over your head, poking at your ears, examining your skull close up. So whenever I've found a barber I like, I build on the relationship, stick to her or him like glue. I want to *know* this person who has learned the map of my head; I talk, ask questions, and even share details of my life, all to forge a lasting bond between us. Ideally I'd like to keep the same haircutter forever, never change; it's painful when I have to.

For instance, just after moving to Vancouver, one day I found myself standing in front of an old style "assembly line" barbershop, impersonal, with twenty barbers working in two rows of ten chairs, just off Robson Street, taking whoever sat down next in their chairs. I watched for a while—it looked soulless but efficient—then took a chance, went in. I sat down with the rest of waiting customers, all reading out-of-date *Sports Illustrated* and *Maclean's* magazines. There was not much talk, just the buzzing of clippers. Then when someone in a raised voice said, "Next," I took the first empty seat, leaving it all up to fate. That's how I met Mario, a soft-spoken Greek of about thirty-five, with a gentle smile and slightly melancholy demeanour. And he turned out to be an excellent barber, skilled at cutting and, equally important, knowing how much to chit-chat or not. For twelve years all was well, till Mario, who had often complained about not being able to get ahead in Canada, started talking of going back to the Old Country. I tried to re-direct him, for purely selfish reasons, advised him to strike out on his own, that no one made good money in a "factory"—but it was no use. Eventually, he packed up and moved back to Greece.

After a lot of searching, I discovered Manni on Broadway, close to my apartment. She was a dark-skinned Baha'i single mom, from Iran originally. We were blissfully together for seven years, and I remained faithful through several inner city moves, traveling further and further across town to keep our relationship strong. But then she, too, decided to move far away. Traumatized, I didn't get my hair cut for many weeks; while thinning on top it grew unaccustomedly long down my neck, blowing in the breeze as I marched in a new purgatorial round of barber hunting.

And finding your barber is something you have to do on your own, a personal chemistry sort of thing. Recommendations from friends just don't work. After Manni, I tried several places with increasingly bad results. My few remaining hairs were becoming a real burden. I'd spend hours driving around town, analyzing shop fronts, skulking past windows to get a glance at the cutters inside, all to "feel" my way to the right fit.

But you can never really tell just by looking. I'd learned that with my first barber, that one in the North End, near St.

John's, whose friendly shop on the corner I ventured into, after trudging round the block several times to build up my courage for my very first *real* haircut. I was thirteen. I knew my parents would be put off at the waste of good money; maybe my father would even get mad at me. That didn't happen often, mostly he was cool and ironic; but occasionally I had infuriated him without even knowing how, once to the point of him throwing a wooden peach crate at me. Still, my teenage haircut plan had to be carried out, whatever the cost, whatever the violence. I had to be me.

With no idea of how much it would cost, and whether I had enough money, I finally entered the barber's realm, looking nervously around for a price list on the wall. There was none. I touched the bills and coins in my pocket, and hoped they would be sufficient.

The barber got out of the chair, motioned me to take the seat. I sat down in his chair, breathed in the various smells of antiseptics, aftershaves, tobacco, the authentic aromas of a real men's barbershop. "What's your pleasure, kid?" the barber asked, casually adjusting the chair's height with his foot.

"Uh...something not too short, maybe kind of Beatle style?"

He snorted, put down his pipe, switched on the clippers: "Don't wanna look like a freak, do you?"

"Well..." I paused.

Without waiting for my answer he moved in closer and the buzzing, louder than at home, began. I was trapped.

"It's n-not really that long, the Beatles' hair, I mean, just a little different at the front, sorta flat." I babbled; he went on cutting, first at the back. I thought I smelled rum on his breath, though it was still morning. Later he nicked my ear; it bled onto my shirt collar, crusted there.

The bill, when it came, took all the money I had. So I left the barbershop empty-pocketed, with a sore ear...and another regulation crewcut, looking, if anything, worse, geekier than after a session with my father. When I got home, my father was in the kitchen. It wasn't a haircut day, so he didn't have his clippers or anything. He was just sitting there smoking and gazing out the window as he often did, quiet, waiting for dinner to be served. He looked up and asked, "What happened to you?" But he knew, of course, the evidence was right there on my head.

On the spot I made up a stupid story, a lie, about a friend persuading me to try Molar's Barber School on Main Street, with their one-dollar cuts by students. It was a great deal, I insisted. And...my friend really wanted us both to do it.

My father laughed shortly, shrugged, then turned back to the window, puffed on his Player's cigarette. It was clear that he didn't believe me...or my imaginary friend. And it hurt, though of course I was lying. I looked out the kitchen window too, into the big green vegetable garden beyond, realized there was no way back to those hateful Saturday haircut afternoons, and felt a pang, like I had lost something.

My dad never laid his hands on my head, ever again, in that intense, knowing way, following its shape to create an A-1 Polish military style brush cut. There was no need to. In fact, being that we were not a touchy-feely family nor a rough-housing-football one, and that apart from the peach box, corporal punishment was not meted out by my father, it turned out to be pretty much the end of any father-son physical contact between us. I had made my choice.

Fool of Cool

In grade eight, the final year of elementary at Holy Ghost, I was hungry all the time, grabbing food when I was out, spending whatever cash I had on fries and hot dogs at Kelekis, Eccle cakes and chocolate bars from the corner store, then coming home to a hearty dinner. Not that I ever told my mother about spending good money on bad food.

"Why you want to go for coffee?" she would say: "To a restaurantee. You can have all you want here." To her, eating out was a crazy activity, as if every dining experience was no more than a nutrition fix without social or other dimensions. As a family we certainly never went out to eat—except on trains to St. Louis, to visit my mother's brother there and his family, when, after twenty or so hours it became a necessity to have sustenance beyond what could be carried, neatly wrapped in humble wax paper and carried in my mother's elegant alligator purse.

Through that school year, smoking was my solace, calming my hunger into a quiet, almost pleasant ache. My father started smoking when he was ten; that's when he became a man officially in the old country. His mother gave him his first carton of cigarettes in Poland as a rite-of-passage, health-enhancing gift on that February 7th birthday in 1926. Smoking, it was believed, soothed the nerves and relaxed the stomach, thereby improving appetite, and hence generally made you robust; these had been well-known medical facts, according to my parents, in those bygone days. I suspect there was also a bit of social pretension that went with the habit, a sign of class, a frivolous though stylish indulgence, really, which only the true *sclachta* (Polish aristocrats) could afford, or pretend to. Maybe that's partly why I craved it. But I also loved the ritual: the anticipation, the slight thrill from buying smokes undercover when underaged ("my dad wants some Players, please"), watching the clerk pull the shiny little box off the neatly stacked shelf, then tossing it over with a package of matches, a knowing look on his face. I didn't care if he knew. I was already outside in the back lane opening the sealed life-affirming pack of smokes, by twisting the dainty red opening band off the clear plastic around the flip-top, freeing the trapped delight inside, that first sweet hit of fresh wholesome tobacco aroma. Then the cool elegance of lighting up, which could be tricky in the wind, making you look like a fool: turning the flip-top back on itself and pulling one cigarette out of the orderly maze of perfect filter heads, flicking your Zippo with that satisfying "click" sound, inhaling that first slightly acrid yet deeply satisfying puff. The soothing aftermath as you let the smoke cascade out of your mouth and nostrils. Pure bliss. Then, later, slipping around the back of the school to have a few more drags at recess, before heading back in, was another beautiful moment, transitory yet fulfilling, a gift in the day.

Sometimes, though, one of the nuns had her eyes on me and I couldn't sneak off; then my constantly growling stomach would turn my thoughts elsewhere, like to the war stories my mother repeated in a seemingly endless loop. These narratives of survival were important at home, the essence of our family history. Not surprisingly, food played a big role in these stories. Nothing, not even a crust of bread, was ever wasted. Thrift was a sacred tribute to the past times when there had been no food: like in the Siberian slave labour camp. One of my favourite stories was about Hanik, whom I had grown up thinking of as one of my many unofficial "uncles." He and his wife had met my parents at the start of the war, and they followed us to the other side of the world, settling down nearby as close family friends.

In the camp where they all spent a forlorn year and a half, workers had to toil every day in order to buy their food. One day's labour logging trees equaled one loaf of bread, or a couple of potatoes. Life was a simple equation: no work, no food.

My parents' countryman, Hanik, woke one morning and decided he'd had enough of his miserable existence. Months of starvation rations, freezing every day in the forest, every night on his flea-infested pallet: no more, he vowed, no matter what they did to him. A once-burly and energetic man with a big appetite, he refused, one icy morning, to budge from his bed.

Shortly, Hanik found himself before the camp Commandant, who, surprised by the insubordination, asked, "What is the problem? Don't you want to eat?"

Beyond despair, Hanik laughed bitterly: "Yes, I want to eat—I'm hungry always. You don't give enough. A man can't work on an empty stomach, you Russian swine. Go ahead, shoot me; I don't care any more."

The Commandant, not unsympathetic (like many of the Russians my parents encountered during their captivity, he apparently was kindly disposed to Poles), seemed touched by this bravado. He called for food to be brought in.

A steaming pot of soup arrived. Hanik said: "What about bread, you bastard, and butter?"

The Commandant gave in: "All right. Today you'll eat well, and then work like a whole platoon."

Next came bread and lots of butter. Hanik ate it all but he was still hungry. "Bread and soup is not a meal," he said. Next came a big bowl of potatoes mashed with pork drippings and fried onions. He finished it. Still he was not satisfied. "That was just a side dish," he declared.

Beginning to lose patience while at the same time amused by this captive worker's gall, the Commandant called for something "substantial." A hearty stew arrived; Hanik demanded beer to chase it: "I'm not an animal," he asserted. He got beer. Hanik ate and ate, and drank and drank, until everything was gone.

"Had enough?" the Commandant inquired.

"For the first time in a year."

"Then get to work, you Polish sonofabitch!"

But Hanik shook his head, burped loudly, and replied, "I cannot."

"What—what do you mean?"

Hanik patted his swollen stomach. "I'm too full to move."

In the afternoon a notice was posted on the commissary bulletin board: Hanik was the only worker to exceed his quota for the previous day, and so had received "special rations." The funny part was that the Russians tried to save face by making Hanik out to be a hero; at least that's what seemed to make my mother laugh each time she told the tale. But what struck me was Hanik's determination, ready to face death for a hearty meal; now that was pretty cool. Maybe that's how you got in wartime—fatalistic, bleakly humorous, devil-may-care.

Wars and disasters were all part of life, something that I had been brought up with from the first words I can remember. Maybe that was the point of my mother's endless fund of repeated tales. It seemed perfectly normal for nations to war against each other. The history of Poland itself was the history of war, after all—war against Russia, Germany, Austria, and so on, in a sort of "if this is Tuesday we must be fighting the X..." perennial pattern.

My mother didn't blame anyone in particular for WWII and her fate, except maybe Churchill for having sold out the Poles to the Communist Russians afterward, so that, for some obscure Bolshevik reason, she could not go back to her village when she tried in the sixties and seventies. In her mythic overriding story of survival, war was 100% natural, a force of Nature, not a matter of evil or morality. That's why she could revile Hitler one minute, the next praise the Nazis for their perfect discipline, elegant uniforms, "blondy hairs," and generally good Nordic looks.

And war did make sense, sort of, if you thought about it. It was like a chess game on an international scale. Country X needed country Y's resources, transportation network, etc., in order to expand its empire, thereby fulfilling its destiny. Making the leap, I realized why Winnipeg was such an important strategic target during the Cold War, and why we practised A-bomb drills in school. The Peg is the actual geographic centre of North America and years ago was a crucial mid-continent transportation hub—a railway capital in the middle of the vast empty prairie, a thousand miles from anything at all. That made us pretty darn important.

But all this speculation about warfare was futile, I realized fairly early on; the promised nuclear war wouldn't be like my parents' tragicomic army days at all. No concentration camps and no commandants, humane or otherwise, to banter with; no displacement, refugeeism, or years of DPdom and "soffering" (as my mother pronounced it) through food and other shortages. Just a searing flash of nuclear light brighter than the sun, then zero, or rather less, the hole in the zero. Nuclear war of nowadays was so much more modern, effective, and efficient, it would destroy the world in mere minutes—now that was progress.

I sometimes pictured a globe, like the one standing in the corner of our homeroom at Holy Ghost, exploding at selected co-ordinates. Winnipeg would be first, then the other "hot spots" would erupt in discrete pinpoints of flame before the whole globe was utterly destroyed in a ball of cosmic fire. No more geography class—my map-making days would be over; though, despite our family history (or maybe because of it?), my passion had never been to record the shifting realities of recent history, the amoebic forming and re-forming of post-WWII countries. What I loved, and what I seemed to be loved for, was the creation of maps of the long-ago past: I was a gazetteer of the Ancient World. That had become my special calling, somehow, under the guidance of Sister Caroline, our kindly, mustachioed history teacher, and now I was recognized as the school's official map-maker. Unlike the other students who apparently did lots of different kinds of homework every night, I spent most of my out-of-class time working on big 4' x 6' maps of the Ancient World, of Alexander's conquests, the Pax Romana, Mesopotamia, and others.

My cartographic career coincided with and was aided by my normally penny-saving mother's aberrant purchase of a brand new *Encyclopedia Britannica* the year before, to help me and my younger brother through school. Going against my father and family friends, who thought spending money on books was insane, especially with library cards free for all, Mom laid out what was big bucks in those days—close to $200—on a complete set. My father scorned our lavishness. Over dinner, his mouth full of Sunday roast chicken, he shook his head: "Guess you can eat your words when you get hungry. Ha."

For my dad the encyclopedia was a collection of pricey books, perhaps even a kind of pretentiousness or showing off to the neighbours that we were educated. For me it quickly became The World, or rather an improved, preferable, self-contained version of the real one, with all of its history, geography, art, science, literature, architecture—everything desirable, in fact—at my fingertips. Real life was mad, after all, nothing but wars, accidents, death, more wars, natural disasters like the Red River flood of not long before. Flux, upheaval, havoc—who wanted that craziness? The two shelves of burgundy-bound books of wisdom in their dark brown wood case provided a refuge for me, a meditative quiet place where the chaotic stream of human existence was ordered in one clear, comprehensible output that I could peruse at my leisure. Here, on thousands of perfectly printed pages, each volume proffered alphabetical solace, wherein the whole range of human experience, everything, made downright sense—not to mention the complimentary hefty World Atlas volume, the scroll projector, and the yearbooks that came as "extras."

Years later, in university, I learned in a shattering scholarly revelation that my edition of these particular "knowledge books," as they were called, like other such publications, was full of inaccuracies and errors. But at the time I first explored them in grade school I was convinced of their accuracy, and I loved the reassuring heaviness of each of the authoritative twenty volumes. And it was out of the *Britannica*'s pricey pages, so rich with words, images, charts, and maps, that I created my cartographic masterpieces—the glorious pageant of Mediterranean history captured on paper in Laurentian pencils' splashy reds, primal yellows, and royal purples. The place names made a mystical music in my head: Babylon, Herculanuan, Alexandria. How colourless and flat, in comparison, were the maps of my own day—and, by extension, the age we lived in. Canada: a big watery pink patch at the top left-hand corner of the global map, with clunky, unpoetic names like Newfoundland, Brampton, Moose Jaw, Abbotsford dotting its bland emptiness.

To make one of my Old World masterpieces, first I copied in proportion the grid on the page of the actual map in the *Britannica*. Then I'd tape a big sheet of art paper—my canvas—up on the wall of my room over the bed, close the door, and turn off the lights. Using the scroll projector, I'd slip part of the map page onto the lit surface where the film normally went, and project it onto the hanging paper. With a fine, hard pencil, I'd trace the contours of the countries and seas, spot the cities and important towns, mechanically reproducing the contents of each gridded section, until the "big picture" took shape.

As I carefully traced the defining lines in the secured darkness of my curtained room, I could almost see Alexander, the youngest conqueror in history, a bronze god astride his horse moving across archaic vistas, traversing vast domains with lightning speed, taking what he wanted when he wanted it, bringing to the Middle East and India the indelible image of the West, of himself, that would grace so many statues alongside Shiva and Buddha.

Later I'd go back over the outline with pens, thickening or feathering them as needed, separating nations and cultures with a stroke, creating the past anew.

I remember just after Christmas planning out a map of the Byzantine Empire and finding myself in a bit of a dilemma. Should I shade in the different countries with solid or washed tinting, or just bold their edges, then add some strokes of solid colour surrounding their names? What would be most Byzantine? That was the question.

I was just entering the school after recess and a secret smoke, when Pete fell into step with me as we brought up the tail end of the kids going back into class. He seemed oddly jumpy. "Did you see him, the black guy?" he asked.

"Huh? You mean like 'Negro'?"

"Yes, he's blacker 'n coal—no kidding." He laughed. "Pretty amazing. I saw him out in front of the school."

"Yeah?" I was mildly curious. This was 1962. I'd only ever seen a couple of real black people in Winnipeg, porters in their uniforms, down around the railway stations on Main Street: CPR at William and CN at Broadway. We'd go to the Starland Theatre for cheaper second run films, then have Boston cream pie and coffee at the Golden Wheel Chinese-Canadian up towards McDermot, and sometimes these porters would be out on the street in their gold-buttoned uniforms, impressive against the backdrop of mostly Europeans and Métis who populated that end of town. There were also a few Jamaican students on the United College downtown campus. I'd seen a group playing in the snow the winter before as I went by on a bus. They were running around in sweaters and white cotton pants, no jackets, laughing like crazy as they slipped and fell in it, looking a little bewildered and out of context against the white covered grounds, shivering with exaggerated gestures, as if they'd never seen snow before.

"Are Jamaicans blacks?" I asked Pete. "I mean, they seem sort of pale brown, some of them. Beige even."

"Nah," he replied knowledgeably. "They're different." But he did not elaborate before going down the stairs for his next class.

For a moment, I felt let down by everything—Pete taking off so quickly, not seeing the superblack guy outside the school, going up the same old creaky stairs I'd climbed a thousand times before—once again I had been robbed of a chance for excitement. Now it would be like every other day, when nothing happened, stuck at my stupid desk.

But I was wrong.

"Richard." It was Sister Augustine, flapping her black-tuniced arms like a huge crow at me from the landing.

"Yes, Sister?" Perhaps without realizing it I had committed yet another obscure transgression, a careless sin that would put me on Purgatory time for a zillion years. You could never tell with nuns.

"I have a job for you, a sort of..."She hesitated. "...*guardian angel* kind of position."

This unexpected reference to guardian angels bothered me. Back in grade five, lovely Sister Lioba had convinced us of the existence of guardian angels in a stunningly simple way. All you had to do, if confronted by the spectre of disbelief in God and his wonders, was to take this easy test: Instead of turning on your alarm clock at night when going to bed, just ask your guardian angel to wake you up at a specific time in the morning. Everybody had a personal, dedicated guardian angel, she explained in her sweet, clever voice, on the job twenty-four hours a day, looking out for your best interests, and you could call on this heavenly creature for help at any time. I called on my angel, and was indeed awakened perfectly, 7:00 a.m. on the dot—though I didn't tell anyone that. For some reason I found the fact of it not gloriously faith-enhancing but instead unnerving, even depressing, like we were all trapped in a Chinese box where nothing was unpredictable or private. So I told no one.

"You've been down to the States, haven't you? Kansas, was it?" Sister Augustine asked, breaking into my celestial thoughts.

"St. Louis," I said, and then in a spirit of map-consciousness added, "in Missouri."

"Yes."

I elaborated: "Through Chicago, on the train, several times over the past few years. My uncle and his family live down there."

"Yes, very good. We're getting a new student, from Los Angeles, for—well, at least part of the term. And I thought you might show him around, take him under your wing, as it were. He doesn't know anyone round here and...you probably met boys like him, in St. Louis." She paused.

"An American," I said. Obviously my broadening travels had matured me in the eyes of authority.

"Yes. Why don't you come by my office at the end of last class today; I'll make sure he's there and you can meet."

"OK." For a moment, the dark creases around Sister Augustine's eyes smoothed out as she smiled. Then she turned and walked up the stairs.

Several times during the day I wondered, why me? Lots of kids went to the States, to Grand Forks and Detroit Lakes in the summer. And anyway, since when did new kids get an assigned companion? What was the big deal?

But when I turned up the corridor to Sister Augustine's office, I understood instantly. This wasn't just any new kid, this was the black guy—"black as coal," as Pete had said. He was about my height and size, but dressed in the most improbable—especially in terms of wintry Winnipeg—outfit: shimmery blue shirt (silk?) under a light blue jacket, shiny gold pants, and navy-blue Cuban-heeled shoes. And he was, as Pete had said, amazingly black. The word "ebony" popped into my head, that dense, light-defeating darkness—so black that the whites of his eyes seemed unnaturally luminous, like light bulbs.

The black kid hadn't noticed me because he was silently practising a dance step in front of the principal's office, prancing around to some secret music in his head in a loose, lanky rhythm, moving like a big elegant Egyptian cat. I saw his hair was oiled down on his head in a modified Elvis duck-tail at the back with a pompadour at the front curved into a fall in the middle, the suppressed kinky curl I associated with black people giving the haircut an undulating though firmly set look. The sleeves of his jacket were rolled halfway up the forearms, a double-cuff length; beneath, his electric blue shirt was open to mid-chest. A thick gold bracelet hung from his left wrist. Most curious of all, the shimmering slim pants seemed to defy gravity, hanging without a belt impossibly low on his hips, buttoned barely above the crotch.

He was really cool.

At that moment, Sister Augustine opened the door of her office and smiled, a quick nervous gnash of long yellow teeth. "Come in, boys."

The black kid whirled around to check me out, bouncing up and down on the balls of his feet, as if he couldn't stand still. He grinned, a dazzle of brilliant Chiclets. I smiled back a bit shyly, and we went into the office, eyeing each other sideways.

"As I said, Richard, Louis is going to be with us—"

I was briefed; Louis' dad was in the U.S. Air Force and had been transferred to Manitoba on some liaison work connected to the North American Aerospace Defense Command, or NORAD. And his parents wanted Louis to go to a private school while the term appointment lasted.

I felt rather shy throughout this info session. The truth was Sister Augustine had made a poor choice of guardian angel. Sure there were many blacks in the "gateway"city of St. Louis, millions, maybe. But I knew nothing much about them, or blacks in general, except what I had seen on TV and in the movies, stuff about how they had suffered persecution and displacement, been slaves, and so on. And, really, I had hardly thought about black people in any context. None of my relatives down in St. Louis—my mother's brother, his wife and kids—socialized with blacks, or had "Negrow" (as they called them back then) friends, and certainly never introduced any to us. The only blacks I'd actually spoken to, a few words here and there, had been the smiling brass-buttoned porters on the trains, going down to St. Louis or coming back.

But I went along with the proposition, being, of course, flattered. Sister Augustine made Louis and me shake hands, and then we were out of school and on the way to my house. I was in the habit of bringing home friends, old and new, thanks to my mother's exaggerated hospitality principle that opened our home to all comers, from beggars to salesmen (encyclopaedia and others).

As we walked, or rather as I trudged and Louis "flowed" down the street in loose-limbed boneless motion, I kept eyeing him sideways, taking in every detail of this dazzling exotic hip kid. The February wind whipped down Charles Street from the north as we turned on it, a wintery reminder of the North Pole. I zipped up my trusty fleece-lined parka. "Jeez, aren't you freezin'?" I asked.

He shrugged, his lips bluish-black in the dimming light of late afternoon. "Nah."

"Bet it doesn't get this cold in L.A."

He laughed for the first time, a soft mellow sound, speaking as if in slow motion. "For...sure...it...don't."

"Don't you have a parka?" We were passing an old *babushka*-swathed woman standing at the bus stop; her eyes followed Louis as if he were from another planet.

"What's a pahk-ah, man?"

"A winter jacket—it snows around here."

"No kiddin? Where'd Eskimos?"

When we got to my place, dinner was already making its way to the table. "You...from St. Louis?" my mother asked my guest. "No," he replied, "California, basically." My father grinned at Louis, and said in fatalistic Polish: "He's going to freeze to death dressed crazy like that."

In the general silence that graced meals at home, we sat down to steaming platefuls of pyrogies. After trying one, Louis asked for some hot sauce; my mother looked blank. "Like, Tabasco or somethin'?" he elaborated. I went to the fridge and got out the *buracki*, a mix of horseradish and pickled beets.

Louis helped himself, dabbing each potato dumpling generously with the tangy purple condiment, as my parents, amazed, watched him.

Over the next weeks, I showed Louis around, took him to some hangouts like Kelekis and then downtown, to the Paddlewheel Restaurant in the Bay, where there was a functional paddlewheel turning in a shallow pool of water framed by some stenciled riverboat scenes, on the top floor of the building, and then Gibson's Billiards, the elegant new pool hall where we shot a few games. He was a natural pool player, loose and lithe around the table—but easily distracted, which is where my chances to win came. After a few of these downtown excursions, he seemed to "feel" his way through the city, finding shortcuts that I didn't even know about, through alleys, as if he carried a primal city map in his head. Capering down those cold concrete streets, all black in face and shiny in fancy clothes, he seemed out of place yet oddly at home against the urban backdrop of the city, a fascinating colourful image.

And Louis started showing me a few things. One day downtown, he said: "Let's go li-ber-ate some clothes, man." I was a little shocked, not having ever shoplifted anything; but he was so matter-of-factly cool about it that I went along without much worry.

You could choose between the Bay or Eaton's, both on Portage, and both with menswear departments handily located on the main floors with easy access to the street, as Louis pointed out. "You dowanna try this in small stores, up on the third floow somewhere. You gotta be in a big space where you can find a blind spot."

"A what?" I asked.

"Some place where the store dicks can't see exactly what you're doin'."

I looked blank.

"Hey, I'll show ya."

We started out in Eaton's. Louis was wearing a raincoat, loose sweater and pants. We shopped together, just looking over the racks to see what was cool. Then he bought a cheap shirt and asked the clerk for a shopping bag. "OK, my man, let's go," Louis said heading out the door. On Portage, he gave me the bag and instructions: "So when we get in the Bay, you bird dog me, makin' sure no store dick is followin'. And be sure to be cool, like no hurry or scurry, just groovin'; that's the most important thing, you know, confi-*dence* (he emphasized the last syllable dramatically). No one will touch you if you got it."

"Bird dog?"

"Yeah, you know, like from twenty feet away, behind me, seein' if anyone's watchin'."

"OK, I think I get it." And so I bird dogged Louis: watching him first picking out a number of items, then going to the change room, coming out with fewer and putting those back on the rack. Next, very coolly, he walked by a sweater display and calmly shifted one then another cellophane-wrapped package into his now-open raincoat, under each armpit, and, stiffly, made for the exit to Memorial Boulevard. There he dumped them into the shopping bag I was carrying, and we headed to the bus stop. He laughed, a flash of blinding white teeth and eyes. "Wish I could get these underthings off, though."

Beneath his baggy sweater and pants—I discovered later, at my parents' place in my room—Louis had two shirts and a pair of brown checked stovepipe pants on. My share of the haul was a black cardigan-style mohair sweater with a shirt-like collar, loose-fitting body, and fancy black buttons along the centre and on the cuffs—a gift. Very cool.

Shoplifting seemed easy in those pre-video-surveillance days, like you could walk into a department store and simply take what you needed—or wanted. But it was more than just petty stealing, more than silky shirts or stovepipe pants. Louis, I realized, inhabited an underworld of secret knowledge, hidden ways. He was a lawbreaker, an outsider. Or was he a super "insider" who knew more about how the world worked than I did? It depended on how you interpreted life. How had he gained his cool wisdom, I wondered? After all, his parents had to be law-abiding straight arrows, being in the Air Force in a big way, and all that.

I never found out how he acquired his thieving ways, or his exquisite sense of style; he remained a creature from another, better world. Maintaining the mystery, Louis never invited me to his home, or to meet his family. He was always alone, separate, grooving to his private inner music, never talking much, mostly responding in monosyllables when answering questions, yet quite content, it seemed, to "hang out," as he called it. He was not at all interested in school, in learning things like history the way I was; he never studied or did any work, as far as I could tell. Maybe that's what being an Air Force brat did to you, moving you from posting to posting, place to place, without rhyme or reason, making you kind of automatic; maybe it was the fact of being black in days when civil rights were just being instituted that made him secretive, private, inaccessible. Or maybe it was just who Louis was.

For a while I imagined he might be under a pledge of secrecy or something, due to his father's NORAD liaison, that being why he did not communicate information about himself and his family. Whatever the reasons, he remained exclusive, solitary, inhabiting a world that was very much his own. Yet I related to him, to his difference that stood out in the Peg like, well, black and white. Being a DP kid myself, a displaced person, a refugee, I did know what it was like to be an outsider; at least we had that silent connection.

One day, over Cokes and shoestring fries at Kelekis, I noticed a rough X scar on his forearm. "What's that?" I asked.

He showed me his other arm, sporting an almost identical cross scar. "Some white kids carved me. Last year."

I was stunned, by the fact of it and by his off-hand delivery. "How come?" I asked.

He shrugged, "For fun, I guess."

"Fun?"

"I was in their 'hood. They grabbed me." He reached into a pocket and pulled out what I recognized from the movies was a switchblade, a black-handled one that made a "snick" sound when you pressed the button and the blade flipped out. "Didn't have this *then*," he said thoughtfully.

I kept learning new things from Louis, not so much about his personal history, but more about the larger world beyond my hometown. For instance, one time Louis brought a stack of 45 records to school and handed them to me; it seemed his record player was broken and he didn't think he'd get another until his dad was sent back to the States. They were all black bands I'd never heard of, with cool names like The Dimensions, The Skyliners, and The Jive Five, their music full of bouncy, vibrant rhythms and energy, unlike the Top Ten hits we got on radio, as typified by Ray Charles and Chuck Berry, which sounded tame after hearing the new stuff.

Then there was the annual Holy Ghost end-of-term outing to Winnipeg Beach, which included the glorious graduating grade eights and also, for some reason, the subordinate grade sevens. Maybe it was just that we needed more bodies than provided by the relatively small class of grade eights so that the whole boardwalk would be opened for one Holy Ghost School day of frolic. It was always in early June, so I guess we got a cheaper rate before the real summer season started in July. We played on our own or in groups during the day, doing the rides—like the rickety wooden roller coaster on which Sharon set a record that day, going twenty-three times. And then we had a wind-up wienie roast right on the beach at the water's edge. You could have as many hot dogs as you wanted, or ham sandwiches, and all the pop you liked. I remember Mitch Novack ate eight hot dogs, for every year he attended, then barfed in the scrub grass. The priests came out with us and oversaw the whole day, men in black that matched the nuns in their similarly black outfits, as if they were all part of the same team.

When we arrived we went straight to the water, to smell that primal stink of life. We took off our shoes, and felt the fine white sand on our naked feet. It was a windy day and the lake was wild, with huge waves because prairie lakes like Winnipeg and Manitoba, though vast in area are shallow, not deeper than fifty feet at the deepest, and hence easily stirred up by stormy weather. Louis and I stayed there for a couple of minutes, trying to skim rocks which the waves swallowed up. But he seemed twitchy: "Come on," he said. "Let's find sumplace...inside."

So we played in the arcade, games like Ball Roll and Tin Pan Alley, and Louis did well in all of them. He was a natural athlete, but not one interested in anything practised in the great outdoors, it seemed. Then we tried the Claw Diggers. I always found these alluring, the glassed-in "boxes" of prizes with glittering items like flashlights with lush purple $10 bills Scotchtaped to them, pocket knives, tools, Zippo lighters, bottles of cologne, cellophaned packs of smokes, and much more—all in a shiny jumble like a container of random Christmas. The trouble was you needed good hand-eye coordination to move the claw-end crane from horizontal and vertical controls exactly over the object of desire. Once you stopped moving it, the claw automatically descended, the three prongs open wide. Once it touched an object, it closed, grabbing on or slipping off from the surfaces of your targeted booty depending on how good a hold it had. That part was in slow motion, heightening the drama of the moment.

I tried for a flashlight wrapped in purple; the claw hooked it at one end, lifted until it was at 90 degrees and, then, dropped it when it became snagged in the pile.

"'S'a fool's game, man," was Louis' verdict. "Heavy batteries in those flashlights; you ain't never goin' get them with this hook. Go for the smokes and lighter stuff; you can at least sell those to your buddies."

He was right, of course; when I focused on the less substantial prizes, less weighty, that is, I did well; that day I clawed six packs of illicit cigarettes and sold them to the other guys and Danuta for almost $5, which kept me going in the arcade for a couple of wild, magic hours, Louis cool and focused at my side.

And that was the last time I saw Louis. A week later, at the Holy Ghost grad rehearsal, he was absent. Not that it was unusual for him to miss big chunks of class time, but it would be weird to miss grad.

After practice, I cornered Sister Augustine, "Is Louis sick today?" I asked.

She started wagging her right hand with its mutilated index finger that was shortened to the first knuckle, her usual gesture when excited or disturbed. The blunt stub used to freak me out, but now I was used to it. She looked surprised by my question: "But—didn't he tell you?"

"Tell me?"

"He—they were shipped out, last Friday, to Germany. Gone."

I was stunned that Louis could have left town without even saying goodbye—to me, his best buddy at Holy Ghost. I felt confused, sure that I would be hearing from him soon, that it must have been some NORAD-related emergency.

Time passed. Grad was a dull success. No word from Louis. Slowly I stopped expecting—what? Anything. In a way, I consoled myself, going without words was cool, Louis-like. Then in the first week of June, I was invited out to a party at Cecile's. She lived with her boozer dad, a train engineer for the CPR. Word was he would be out of town, on the Vancouver run. And Pete said there would be lots of beer, a twelve-pack of Labatts. It sounded promising.

Before heading out, I spent a few minutes posing in front of the mirror. I was looking good: in a fine corduroy windbreaker, black with delicate gold vertical stripes, a gold shirt underneath, a gold chain bracelet I had picked up in a pawnshop, black pants riding low down, and black Cuban heels.

I rubbed a big squeeze of Brylcreem into my hair, slicked the back parts down and even past my ears, bringing them together at what I hoped was the absolute centre line with my comb, in a perfect duck's ass. Then I tried to form the pompadour at the front, shaping it up and then folding both sides down to the middle, in that sulky way that Louis and a lot of pop singers wore it. The only problem was that my hair had zero body, so the pompadour kept falling, flopping over my forehead, hanging almost to the eyes, long and sleekly downward in a spiral. Still, overall, it was pretty cool—especially if I held my head just slightly to one side, the way that Louis used to.

Cecile let me in, grinned, cute in a miniskirt, and then looked me over a bit quizzically. I walked into the living room where the girls, Helen, Christine, Danuta, Wanda, were dancing with each other to the sounds of The Kingsmen's "Louie, Louie" coming out of a portable record player. I thought of Louis again, how he'd disappeared, how cool he'd been.

The guys were hanging back, smoking, sucking on beers. Pete saw me first, and everything seemed to slow down for a moment as all of them looked at me, checking out my outfit. I rocked back and forth on my Cuban heels, lit a Matinée.

Then Pete said: "Hey, man, lotsa grease! Is that a pyrogy on your forehead?"

And they all laughed.

FAT GIRL

In grade eight at Holy Ghost School she was the one who always got hit by the baseball or basketball—any airborne thing, it seemed—and usually started bleeding, in a good-natured sort of way. Bleeding and smiling: that's how I remember Danuta, a big goofy grin and the reddest blood streaming down her face. Then when people ran up to see if she was really hurt, she'd laugh loudly but self-consciously, as if she didn't know how to handle such a moment of awkward celebrity.

Danuta, the Polish version of Donna, was a common name in Winnipeg's North End in those days, the sixties. Our Danuta was the class clown throughout the years I attended the same home room, the alternately funny and pathetic Fat Girl. Not that anyone in class called her that to her face. Most of the time we just called her "Doughnut," thinking it a clever wordplay on her name and roundness. But we also called her "ball magnet," because of the way she attracted identified flying objects. We used to joke about it. To liven up any PT period on Thursday afternoons, all you had to do was put Danuta on the playground, anywhere, and, sure enough, if a ball was flying around—smack. Like fate.

The first time I saw it happen, Danuta was playing dodge ball with half a dozen other grade eight girls, all of them in burnt umber and grey school uniforms. It was one of the first warm days in May. I watched her lurching left, then right, framed against the pale Tyndall stone of the church at the western end of the playground. She laughed like crazy when the ball came anywhere near her. That's what first caught my attention, that wild laugh; I was in a baseball game on the other side of the playground, out in left field, when the raucous sound of it made me turn away from the action of the game.

As I looked on, Danuta got trapped between throwers. She was stopped in mid-dodge, frozen in an absurd caricature of indecision, when the ball took a perverse bounce at her feet and flew up. Splat: her nose blossomed into a crimson peony.

But her ball-magnetism didn't prevent Danuta from joining in games. Though not the athletic type, not at all nimble on her feet or good with her hands, she nevertheless was always up for whatever fun activity was happening. She loved to play. That was the special quality about her, a kind of crazy, rollicking energy and gung-ho enthusiasm; she wasn't your usual quiet, shy, hovering-in-the-background kind of fat girl.

Sometimes Danuta was even trying to *catch* the ball that bonked her, rather than avoid it. That's what happened when she tried out for the girls' softball team. The culprit was a pop fly. Even now I can see the not-so-soft ball flying through the sky, cutting an arc in the bright prairie sky with its dramatic biblical cloudscape, reaching the apex of its trajectory, momentarily fixed at that high point, almost invisible, then coming down fast, falling, gravity-yanked earthward—bopping Danuta right in the face.

I had hit the ball. As the putative coach of the girls' team, I batted it out, one of many, during a tryout exercise. Danuta was standing in right field, but not far out, glove flopping awkwardly in her hand. I watched the action unroll like a slowed film-clip. First, the impact, a moment of profound stillness, then her body gracefully sagging to the ground.

There was something uncanny about it all. As soon as I heard that woody "thunk" of bat on ball, I knew it was going to hit the Fat Girl—as if her much-punished nose and the baseball were lining up in a cosmic convergence, a mystical Zen-archery kind of thing: it was inevitable, even necessary that these two unconnected things, one so hard and one so soft, should painfully collide. In the split second before impact, I even had the illusion that Danuta's nose was a beacon flashing out a secret code that was guiding the ball down, down to its fleshy landing site.

That was how our relationship started. We'd known each other as kids in the neighbourhood and in and around school. But before the incident I'd pretty much ignored the Fat Girl, especially the last couple of years—part of my general cool guy attitude. But then everything changed. I hit the ball. It flew through the air and hit her. She fell down. I ran over to where she lay on the ground, offering a Kleenex to sop up the blood.

I was worried about hitting her. I was also hugely embarrassed to be so publicly paired, even for a moment, by accident, with the Fat Girl.

"You OK?"

"I guess..." she sobbed. Or laughed, I couldn't tell.

"I..."

The other tryouts for the girls' team, looking weirdly formal in their parochial school togs, ran up, huddled above our heads, cutting off the sun. They buzzed with obvious details about the accident: "Rick *hit* her." "Like a guided missile!" "It flew right in her face."

By now my own face was getting hot. Danuta was quiet except for some sniffling, dabbing her nose with the now-dirty Kleenex, making the tissue redder and redder as she looked up at me.

"I...uh—" Desperate, I looked around for a diversion. Through the knee socks and tunics I spotted lovely Sister Lioba in her severe black Benedictine habit, my former grade five home-room teacher and current geography instructor—my one and only love object—marching straight for our little knot of concerned humanity, a no-nonsense scowl on her perfect heart-shaped face. Tall, elegantly thin, and graceful, she moved like a black-robed dancer across the playground.

"Look," I said, increasingly aware of the scene this was causing, "I didn't mean to—"

"No, it's my fault. I always get in the way..." Danuta explained matter-of-factly.

"Oh, yeah?" I muttered, not understanding but glad to be let off the hook so easily.

As I crouched by her, I saw Danuta's hair was not the mousey brown I remembered, but a deep hue of gold; it lay thick and rich, curling round her neck. Her eyes, too, I noticed, weren't the everyday brown I remembered but hazel flecked with bronze, and I got the weird impression that they were always different.

She shuddered, taking a deep breath, and I saw her breasts shift; as the tunic yawned wide at the top, its movement opened her blouse and exposed a lush pink flesh-zone from neck to upper chest.

By then Sister Lioba, the PT instructor, on top of being geography teacher and vice principal, was fluttering over us, snapping out orders to Sharon and Christine to go get help, shooing off the other idly curious girls, efficiently clearing the decks for whatever action needed to be taken in this emergency. Her scowl, I was surprised to see, wasn't for me, the perpetrator, but for my victim. She snapped at Danuta: "What now? Can't you do anything right?"

"I...I was trying to catch...the ball."

Sister Lioba sighed, an exasperated little sound that left her delicate frame like a trapped dove released heavenward. Her long white fingers fluttered. Looking at her from the side, out of the corner of my eye, I noticed her breasts, too, under the sheath of black wool that armoured her from neck to waist over her jersey. Or should I say, I took note of that part of her chest and saw it sort of heave (or what I romantically imagined was "heaving," having read widely) with a certain kind of round swelling action.

"Danuta, why must you always be drawing attention yourself?" our angelic teacher demanded.

The bleeding Fat Girl immediately flipped back to tears. This was an unfair attack, and I felt sorry for her. It wasn't as if she had done anything to put herself in the spotlight or stage the event; it was an accident! The ball magnet thing was just a joke, after all, and Danuta had always appeared to be guileless, without cunning or anything hidden, with her somewhat unusual self all out there on the surface.

As I looked down at her, I noticed her face was actually pretty, or at least it radiated the effect of prettiness; certainly it wasn't the face of a typical Fat Girl. But it was hard to say just how pretty she was; her features were difficult to focus on. They kept changing, lines and angles shifting in a bewildering pattern, as if mirroring a kaleidoscopic range of moods.

For a moment, stuck there close to the ground between Danuta and Sister Lioba, I was transfixed by an awareness of female presence: by Danuta's surprising close-up prettiness, so incongruous with her Fat Girl rep, and Sister Lioba's alluring femaleness, so at odds with her world-renouncing nun role. (Bride of Christ—what the hell did that mean, anyway?) The air around my troubled head throbbed with significant sexual differences. I guessed that Sister Lioba had breasts, and, presumably, other female parts; I had speculated on this subject often in the geography classes she so capably taught. But holy moly—

So many breasts. Sex was the final frontier, the great puzzle, that one remaining barrier between me and the Mysteries of Adulthood. At fourteen, sex was always on my mind, as lusting after a head-to-toe-habited nun must attest. It dominated my uncertain young life, everywhere manifesting its allure, daily rearing its snake-like head.

Women were so...*different* is what it came down to. How could you ever get close enough to even understand them?

Yet how could you not want to? My heart thumped, blood banged in my ears. I put my hand down to the ground to steady myself, and it skidded on the playground's gravel surface, grazing the skin on my palm. I saw a spot of blood there.

Then Danuta was up on her feet, and after another Kleenex or two, baseball practice resumed. We all trudged back to our places, me at home plate. The other tryouts predictably stumbled through their stuff while the Fat Girl sat on the bench, a little pale and wan, watching me.

As I banged out easy grounders and pop flies to the team hopefuls, I was uncomfortably aware of Danuta's eyes on me, and for a moment had a sense of spooky déjà vu, that this had occurred somehow, somewhere before. But, no, I decided. Nothing had even happened, so, logically, it couldn't have happened before. I had accidentally hit the Fat Girl with a baseball, but she was OK. No big deal. I didn't much care for baseball, anyway, and was just doing my duty as the only grade eight guy free from important athletic commitments to coach the girls' team. End of story.

I deliberately didn't think about Danuta at all for the next week, until I literally bumped into her during PT, as we both rounded the corner of the gym.

"Ooops!" I said, instantly embarrassed. "How's it going?"

She laughed, squinting up at me, a face full of sun. "OK, I guess. Like a nosebleed."

I laughed back; that was one of my mother's favourite expressions, maybe a generic Polish saying, that meant: "it's going, though not very pleasantly."

"Right," I said. "Know what you mean." There was a long pause, as I rocked back and forth on my heels. "Sorry you didn't make the team."

"That's all right. I'm not exactly Babe Ruth, whoever she was. I was just trying out, you know, for fun."

"It's 'he'—he was a guy, the great Babe."

"Oh, yeah? Really?" Danuta was unlike other girls, not at all guarded and self-protecting; she didn't seem to know how to protect herself, in fact. I didn't understood her, but felt oddly relaxed standing there beside her, talking.

Then, in a flash of teenage paranoia, I knew something was terribly not right. A hundred eyes were fixed on us—on me with the Fat Girl, standing there, yakking away and grinning like an idiot, having the time of my life, apparently.

"Well, gotta run," I blurted.

"Right." She flushed a little, looking disappointed at our talk ending so abruptly, or perhaps disgusted because she sensed the reason for my panic. Delicate spots of red crept up her cheeks to warm her what now appeared to be golden eyes.

And run I did, literally, to the baseball diamond where the girls who had made the team waited for my lacklustre tutelage. I ran to distract myself from thinking about how much I sort of liked Danuta; the gravel crunching beneath my feet blotted out my conflicting thoughts.

But wait a second—

What the hell was going on? How could I actually *like* the Fat Girl? I mean, I wasn't a Fat Guy, after all. So what could be the attraction? Maybe I was *abnormal* or...*pre*-verted.

On the way home that day, John Slezak, my sometime friend most-time enemy, fell in with my confused steps.

"How's the girlfriend, Rick? 'Dough-nut-ta'?" He laughed a malicious, nasty laugh.

"Get lost, Sleazy-ak."

Today, like most days, John was working hard at being my nemesis. I understood and respected this. After all, he and I were locked in mortal combat for the coolest-guy-in-grade-eight title, stuck in an inevitable nothing-personal pattern of competing young guys keen to outclass each other whether in grades, girls, or games. At times I hated him nevertheless.

"She's hot, that Doughnut."

"Whaddaya mean?" I played along, not believing him, yet willing to listen to anything that had to do with sex.

"Desperate, you know, fat ones are, for any...attention. I hear—"

"Hey, go piss up a rope. You know zip." What had he heard?

John ignored my jibes. "The way you two were snuggling up, there, in front of the gym—real cute. North End sweethearts."

"Jealous? She's really your type, come to think of it. Isn't she, Sleazeball? More bounce to the ounce."

And so it went, blinding exchanges of wit all the way down the block until we parted at Charles Street, turning our separate ways home.

Could it be true? It made a kind of unhappy sense, that a Fat Girl would be, well, more accommodating, more willing to put out, than a Nice Girl or a Beautiful Girl. What else did she have to offer?

Next day in geography class I continued to wonder about the "putting out" business, as Sister Lovely Lioba lectured us on the Canadian Shield. She stood at the front of the room in her blackly null-and-void habit that blended with the chalk-dusty blackboards, her slender long-fingered hands emphasizing the points she was making. It sounded so protecting—a vast rocky girdle enclosing most of Canada at the middle of the Continent. Nothing could penetrate the mighty Precambrian Shield. My favourite nun radiated such serene knowledge and confidence that I felt great to be Canadian: inviolate, strong, and free. I drifted in an adulatory daze. Sister Lioba's soft voice was melodious yet passionate; her eyes blue as jays. A beautiful woman who had sacrificed her beauty and sexuality, had adopted a uniform designed to obviate both—what a mystery. There wasn't much flesh on her; what you could see, I mean, only face and hands, really, and those parts were luminous, as if her soul was shining through the restraining skin. She would not be putting out for anyone, and that was a great pity, or a triumph of the spirit, depending on your point of view.

My daydreaming came to a sudden end when the bell went. As I was leaving, Sister Lioba caught my eye: "Richard, just a moment."

I waited, embarrassed, as she wiped off the board and gathered up her books, thinking perhaps she'd read my thoughts through some sneaky nun trick.

"Walk with me," she commanded, heading for the door, en route to the mysterious nunnery on the street that bordered the school ground on the north side.

"Sure."

As we went down the hall, with me awkwardly trying to fall in with her sprightly step, she adjusted her wimple with one hand, shaking her head daintily to help the fit; her long headdress curved through the air in a languid black S.

"Have you decided about next year, where'll you go for high school?"

"Not really, not yet." I didn't want to think about that. Finishing grade eight was a monumental step; the summer would be my last blast of childhood, I sensed. Next September loomed as a vast dark unknown continent on the horizon of my future.

She frowned: "I'm...thinking of putting you down for the St. Paul's scholarship."

"Really?" That was the Jesuit-run high school downtown, for boys only, prestigious and selective, the next step for any smart Catholic kid on the road to a complete education.

"Yes..."

"That's great, I guess." I knew John and some of the others would be going, those from super-devout families willing to scrimp and save in order to pay the tuition.

She hesitated. "You do have a bit of a, how shall I put it, an attitude problem, though."

I remembered how she used to highlight my grade five report cards with unblissful comments like "can do better" and "not trying very hard." And I protested: "But I like school."

Sister Lioba stopped in mid-stride and turned to face me, her blue eyes shiny with conviction and her face aglow. "You like what *you* like, and don't try hard at what you don't. Life's not like that, Richard. It's not meant to be easy."

I nodded enthusiastically, basking in the nearness of my lovely teacher, though I wasn't totally sure about her stern long-suffering perspective.

"But St. Paul's could change things, turn you around."

"Oh—"

"The Jesuits are great teachers, you know. And you don't want to go to a 'public'"—she made it sound like a dirty word—"school, do you?"

"I guess...not."

We were already at the residence, stopped in front of the six-foot gate. For a moment we stood there silently. Then Sister Lioba told me she would pray for me to help me make the right commitment, and disappeared behind the tall wooden fence.

Whereas before I had been dreading grade nine, now I was filled with inspiration. St. Paul's was my goal; my spirit cried out for higher knowledge, to be on the right path and fulfill my beautiful mentor's vision.

The image of Sister Lioba haunted my steps as a typically late spring turned into the usual short, hot summer in the Peg. She was a symbol of all that was best in humankind, I decided, someone who had dedicated her pure life to helping others and to spirituality. I realized that I wanted to dedicate myself to something meaningful, too, follow a great truth—and here was my chance.

But I also started dreaming about her, I mean, in miniskirts and flimsy almost-see-through "religious" garments, coming out of the sky like an angel, fluttering down to my bed.

Yet...at the same time I also dreamt of Danuta and took to walking past where she lived. It was only a block or two out of my way. The summer nights were long, and we, me and the guys, were restless, endlessly walking the city streets in the dark. After dinner, John, Stan, and I, and usually a few of the others, played ball on the Holy Ghost grounds, killing time until the sun set. We waited for the sheltering darkness so we could light up our illicit cigarettes (Du Maurier, for that elegant look), perched on the cool metal bars like a murder of ungainly crows, blowing smoke at the rising moon. We talked about girls we knew, told stories, and gleaned whatever "facts" we could about sex. Like everyone at that age, we were trying to sort out the bullshit from the bits of Crucial Information.

For instance, I wasn't surprised to hear that women's breasts were joined down the middle; that's why they look so stuck-together in low-cut dresses. But I was a little disturbed to find out that all women the wide world over had their periods at the same time; that was eerie. (Not that we really understood what "periods" were, exactly.) And so it went; the nuns had protected us well from the distracting effects of sex education. We were an ignorant bunch, the boys and I. Our teachers could have been proud.

Then, frustrated in our sex speculations, we roamed the North End streets like purgatorial punks. At some point, we'd stop by Kelekis Restaurant for their famous skinny shoestring french fries from the take-out window. One or two of the three Kelekis sisters were always on hand, working the till, dealing out smiles and cheerful chat for free.

After dousing our wax-paper bagged fries with salt and vinegar, we'd stroll down to the river under Redwood Bridge. By the water the night was sultry and mysterious, not like the bright dry bare prairie days; the darkness seemed full of possibilities. Not that anything ever happened. We were hot and horny, but too young to do anything about it, and our frustration infused our interactions with an edgy energy. Sometimes, when the kidding got too raw, there would be fights (usually between John and me) for no reason we could remember by next morning. But mostly we sat around smoking and talking, getting back to what girls really had between their legs. One by one, we left as the night dragged on, depending on curfew times and boredom limits. Finally, alone, I'd turn homeward, too, heading down the dark luminous streets full of normal enough longings that collided with a hoard of bizarre sex "facts."

Many of the houses I passed were screened by blooming lilac bushes, purple or white; their rich perfume, so much stronger in the dark, led me on, reminding me, for some reason, of Sister Lioba. I wondered what her original name might have been. Bernice? Helen? Jane? Nuns had nun-names—these mostly being male, like Bernard, Augustine, and, occasionally even non-male ones like Lioba. Maybe they took those of holy folk they felt a special kinship to. Or maybe nun names were assigned. Would the assignees still hang on to their true names, somehow, the ones they had been born with? Would they be written down someplace, kept secretly in a special book locked in a vault?

I asked a few adults, got some strange looks back, and eventually abandoned the question. But if I could not discover my mentor's true name at least I could find out the significance of this particular one, "Lioba," which was, after all, a pretty weird name that had to mean something special. So I went on a scholarly quest to the main library on William Street, fortress-like with its imposing blackened old stone facade. On the well-stocked shelves of the Religion section, I found several *Lives of Saints*, and, eventually, information on my special one. The original Lioba was born in 700 AD, I read, in Wessex, England, and died in 780, in Mainz, Germany, after being canonized in 770. The English evangelized Germany back then, starting in 748. At the request of Bishop Boniface of Crediton (later Saint Boniface), Abbess Lioba was sent out in charge of thirty nuns who were designated as support workers for the missionary cause.

These nuns had to be hard-working, well-informed, and educated, which was stipulated as including Latin. It sounded like Lioba was a perfect role model for her troop: "always smiling, generous, and intelligent." She is also described as "beautiful in person" (just like my love object). According to the books I searched, some of her letters to Boniface survive, demonstrating her "keen intelligence" and "delightful" personality. I didn't see the letters, but from what I read it was clear Lioba and Boniface had an unusually close professional relationship and friendship. They were ardent correspondents while apart in separate countries. Once both worked in Germany they were apparently in contact every day, either physically or by letter, until Boniface died. He even sought to break burial tradition by stipulating that they, a man and a woman, were to be buried side by side in his monastic enclosure. This was an unheard-of request. And, although initially followed, a few years later Lioba was disinterred and moved to a different cemetery by church authorities so as not to promote a potential scandal.

On one of my usual treks home from the river, away from the lights of Main and Selkirk streets, it occurred to me that although the first Lioba had become famous in her own day, celebrated widely for both brains and beauty, hers was also a sad story—of the unrequited love variety. She and Boniface, living so intimately for decades, in a foreign land, among strangers, as colleagues, friends—surely there was more to it than that. Would this be the fate of the current Lioba, some version of unrequitedness? Yet her purity was beautiful, of course, something to revere.

Past the parcels-to-Poland joint I went, pondering the nature of Platonic love, by the drugstore, round the corner—and found myself smack in front of Danuta's.

And she was there, an unlikely figure on the steps of her parents' white stucco bungalow with pink trim, the yard hedged with bushes and trees that almost hid her from view.

A little surprised because it was so late, I stopped. "How's it going?"

She stood up and came to the gate, up to me, a smile on her shape-shifting face: "I've been babysitting all night; came out to see the stars."

We both looked heavenward. Orion was right above, the three down-angled stars fixing his loins in a glittering line of light.

"Want to sit down?" She waved an arm at the steps. I saw her arms and legs were bare, that she wore a nightie, as if she'd just risen from bed.

"Sure." The gate clicked behind me. I walked to the steps, sat on the top one. Danuta followed and sat down next to me with a sigh. Her closeness reminded me of the ball incident in the schoolyard, how acutely aware I'd become of her body at that time. Now I couldn't think of anything to say.

My arm on the side away from her brushed up against a large peony bush with blooms so heavy they lolled like hanged men's heads. For distraction, I bent over to smell one of the buds that had almost burst through its green sheath, and caught an ancient rose-like scent. In the moonlight I tried to make out the bud's glistening whorls of impacted fleshy folds, to see if it was still sticky with ants.

Peonies were my favourite, the most exotic bloom of prairie summer. While other flowers, like marigolds and daisies, seemed merely functional, the big splashy peonies appeared in the garden as special, flowers from another and more exciting planet—brilliantly coloured aliens trapped in a monochromatic one-dimensional reality.

I looked around; we were enclosed on all sides by bushes which transformed the yard into a secret garden.

Danuta spoke, as if reading my mind: "Don't worry, no one will see you, sitting here with the 'Fat Girl' in the dark."

"Whaddaya mean?"

"Are they calling me something else these days?"

"No—ah, I mean, they're not calling you anything."

She looked away, and after a moment said: "I don't care."

"Good."

"I mean, I'm not really fat."

"Right."

"In the head, I mean—that's where people are really fat."

"Yeah, I—" This I could not follow, didn't want to; I felt as if she was trying to pin me down and choose sides, declare myself as her friend or something.

"Wanna smoke?" I offered after a few moments of silence, whipping my pack of Du Maurier out of my breast pocket, thumbing the flip-top and popping a couple of filter-tips up with a graceful flick of my wrist.

"No thanks, I don't."

I lit up and blew smoke at Orion. Somehow we started talking again more naturally, on other, more pleasant matters—

grade eight gossip, who was crazy about whom, that kind of stuff. We were, after all, the graduating class, the only ones who mattered at our school that year.

We talked and talked. The sky filled with spiraling stars and the night air with rich scents. Nothing disturbed our hidden garden. Beyond the hedges the city slept. As if by magic, we weren't even bothered by the usual big-as-bees Manitoba mosquitoes, at least not any I noticed. I could smell Danuta's skin, or maybe I just felt the magnet of her flesh drawing me. How strange, I thought, to be here with the Fat Girl.

That night was the first of many such encounters on the steps during that summer. Our meetings weren't predictable, though; sometimes Danuta was there, sometimes not. But I seemed to sense beforehand if she would be, as I came down the hot dark pavement. By an unspoken agreement, these meetings remained private, between us, which well suited my petty soul. I didn't want John and the others, anybody, to know I was spending time with the Fat Girl. I wasn't sure what her motives for keeping quiet were, but I was grateful for them.

Then, one night in August, it happened. I remember every detail, how it felt from minute to minute. It was hot and humid, past midnight, the kind of night when you're in a sticky dream, groping puppet-like in the darkness, all the happenings round you and your movements beyond your control.

I was in shorts and a T-shirt, Danuta was in a cotton nightie again. We were talking intently, as usual, eyes locked, side-by-side on the steps, very close. At the back of some empty unzoned space in my mind, I recalled that gravitational moment when the ball I had batted struck Danuta: saw the blood, her falling in a languid double-curve to the ground, the image repeated, caught in a loop of endless memory.

The next moment we were kissing, my hand snaking its way into the wide-open V of her pink nightie's neckline. Her skin was cool, silken, not at all what I'd imagined. My fingers moved on, exploring her round breast which fit my hand exactly, until I found the small bud-like nub of nipple. My fingers stopped there; the nipple swelled, getting full, round, and hard in an instant, doubling and more in size, as if by an astonishing conjurer's trick, until it felt hugely big in my unseeing darkness.

A new world of flesh was incarnate in my eager fingers. I was awed at the discovery that everything can change in a moment, in a sigh or the twist of two fingers—that the body had a vital life of its own, uncontrolled by the mind.

I didn't sleep that night, troubled by big questions. Were we, Danuta and I, now "boyfriend" and "girlfriend," or were we still just "friends"? And if that was the case, should one feel up one's friend, and would a friend put out for another friend? And what about my other friends, the guys on the monkey bars? Could I tell them? Round and round I went, until the birds started their territorial songs at 4:30 a.m.

When we met again at our usual time a few nights later, Danuta wasn't wearing a nightie but rather blue jeans and a red tank top. When I sat down, she said: "Let's go for a walk—I've been cooped up here all day, in this heat."

"I dunno, where to?" This was it, what I had been dreading all summer, my secret Fat Girl life was about to be revealed.

"Holy Ghost? Maybe there's somebody still around; we could hang out."

"How about just a walk?" *In the opposite direction*, I almost added; Danuta was going public about us, and, though I knew deep down that she was right, I didn't want her to. Everything would be spoiled.

"Kelekis?" she countered.

I hesitated, then gave in with a fatalistic shrug. We walked into the night together, side by side, step by inevitable step. Of course, everyone was there, girls and guys together, at our neighbourhood hangout.

Danuta and I stepped out of the darkness into the circle of light the restaurant front gave off on Main Street, and all eyes turned on us. The girls looked interested, the boys surprised. Was it possible that Danuta and I were an item, or were we arriving together by chance? For a moment my little world stood still, everyone and everything in a freeze-frame.

Then John laughed, like a dog barking. "Ha! Been havin' fun, Ricky? Lookin' for the hole in the doughnut, eh?"

"Shuddup," I warned. "You're cruisin' for a bruisin', Sleazoid."

Everyone watched, and I knew he couldn't resist. John's gloating face beamed like a greasy neon sign.

I glanced at Danuta, worried about how she was taking this. But she appeared calm, a smile on her face, as if she knew something I didn't. At that moment I saw her the way you sometimes can really see a person you know very well without the dulling aura of familiarity, fresh, as if for the first time—how I'd seen her at the dodge-ball game at the beginning of summer.

Now, in August, Danuta was different, not "fat" exactly but still sort of larger-than-life, a big blonde girl. Big but sort of beautiful. Her features were heightened, somehow, as if highlighted with a magic pen. Lips full and lush with lipstick, hair like molten gold, skin bronzed from summer sun. I noticed that the delicate blond hairs on her naked arms and shoulders glistened, giving her a penumbra of silken light.

A word popped into my head, a word I had read in a forbidden novel but never understood, even after checking it in the dictionary: "voluptuous." To my ear it was a fascinating term: I felt it sounded like what I thought it meant. But though I knew its denotative designation as a pleasing combination of "sensuous," "fleshy," "pleasure seeking," and "luxurious," its connotative meaning had so far eluded me.

Now John was whispering to Stan and Larry and Pete, and they all sniggered. Then he said out loud, "I wanna ask you something, Rick." And he laughed again.

He walked up to us, until his big shiny red face was just inches from mine.

"I..." He was laughing so hard he gasped for breath. "How does that, ah, 'ball magnet' stuff work in the dark?"

My fist caught John on the side of the face with a nice solid "ka-thunk" sound, followed by an even more satisfying "ka-kung" noise as my arch-enemy slammed into the telephone pole behind him. Then we were down, on the sidewalk, rolling in the dirt, hammering each other with our fists. I felt none of the blows.

The guys goaded us on, the girls squealed, a rain of hot soggy french fries fell on our heads—"french flies," I thought idiotically—cars on Main Street slowed, stopped, honked their horns. Then, after what seemed both a very short and very long time, a siren wailed in the distance, getting ominously closer.

The next day, at 2:00 p.m., I was standing shamefaced in front of Sister Lioba, having been summoned by phone. Her office was Spartan: blank white walls with grey trim, a plain maple desk, a straight-backed chair behind it. The only ornamental touches were a framed picture of the Holy Ghost (that is, of the dove that represents it) on the wall to my right, and a wooden apple on the desk. A big replica Macintosh, or maybe Spartan, the apple was yellow-gold on top shading to rich red on the bottom, with a tiny black stem; a faint horizontal line in the middle marked where the two halves fit. The only spot of colour in the room, it drew the eye like a magnet.

For an unbearable moment Sister Lioba had a sad, stern look on her pretty face, her mind clouded by bad thoughts about me. She studied some papers on the desk, and stared at me. "A...brawl, at a restaurant; is that right, Richard? And you started it?"

"Not really a brawl, more a...fight." Somehow this distinction was important.

"With girls, at 11:00 last night..." She sighed. "The police came by this morning. Do you know how this makes us—Holy Ghost School, the parish—look? Almost our whole graduating class, supposedly the best students, fighting, like...delinquents."

Sister Lioba was in charge of the graduating ceremonies, now tainted by this scandal; every word of her disappointment broke my heart. "I'm sorry, it sort of—I dunno—had to happen. One of those things."

For a long moment she sat silent. "And what about September, Richard? Do you want to wind up," she paused, "at St. John's for grade nine?"

Despite its saintly name, St. John's was a public high school further north in the North End with a reputation, in our limited parochial school purview, for being wild and on the rough side. That was where Danuta and the other girls, hundreds of girls, actually, would be, not like at St. Paul's, which was for boys only. I hesitated: "I haven't really thought much about it."

"Well, it's up to you, of course, whether—"

A tapping sound behind me interrupted the inquisition. I turned to see Sister Augustine, the principal, at the glassed office door, beckoning Sister Lioba. She stood up: "Just a minute," and went out.

Maybe it was more late-breaking bad news about last night, though I could not imagine what that might be. Or perhaps they were about to compare notes. I felt trapped; life was full of choices, big important decisions to make. I stared blankly at the desk, my legs pinned to the floor in front of it.

Out of curiosity, for a moment's distraction, I picked up the wooden apple. It was warm, and fit perfectly in my palm. I lifted the lid. Inside was a spinning top divided into segments, numbered one to six, each with a coloured race horse in full gallop above the number—red, green, blue, yellow, pink, and orange. Near the centre, each segment had a tiny scooped-out half-circle to catch the white glass marble, the size of a pea, that now rested in the number three position. Dead centre was the spinner, a stiff red nipple sticking up.

Between my thumb and forefinger, I tweaked the spinner. What a weird thing to find on Sister Lioba's desk, a gambling toy. How had it come to her? I looked more closely. Below the horizontal line on one side was a sticker, a maple leaf over a banner that read "souvenir," and beneath that, in bigger, bolder letters, "Niagara Falls, Canada." A memento of a trip, maybe, from her pre-nun existence?

Then it hit me. The apple was a sign, maybe from the Holy Ghost. Instantly I spun the top: instinctively going odd for St. John's and even for St. Paul's.

The tiny marble danced round for a moment, clattering, then landed on number one. Hmmm. I spun again: five this time. I spun a third time, so hard the marble almost jumped out of the apple—and landed finally on number three. I put the apple down, as Sister Lioba's habit swished through the door behind me.

She sat down: "So? What are we going to do about all this...bother?"

"I'm sorry, really, for everything; I want to go to St. Paul's, the scholarship." I was Catholic enough to know when I was being tempted. A gambling apple was obviously the Devil's plaything; I would go in the opposite direction it indicated.

Sister Lioba smiled; her pale face, framed by the stark white/black headdress, softened back into its angelic aspect. Now she radiated purity and love. I could see she was relieved, and I was so glad I'd made the right decision.

She looked me straight in the eye, hers sparkling with absolute conviction: "You know, Richard . . . I believe you may have a special future. With us."

I felt our souls brush. I was so happy.

Sister Lioba smiled beneficently, but looked a little agitated at the same time. Impatiently she waved her arms, looking around the barren room. "We need to...commemorate this." Then she grabbed up the red apple off the desk and held it out to me.

"Isn't it the student who should give the teacher an apple?"

She grinned. "Take it. Life is full of surprises."

"Thanks." I could feel the warmth of her fingers on the bright red wood.

"Richard," she said, being serious again. "I'm sure you'll find the answers you need. Goodbye."

And that, sadly, was the last time I saw Sister Lioba. By the fall she was mysteriously gone. No explanation—the nuns said only that a family matter had taken their colleague back home. That's the way things were in religious orders. Not really open to public scrutiny. Nuns and priests came and went, without explanation. In this case a cloud of vague suspicious speculation hung over the parish for a time, then slowly dissipated.

And, in a way, despite being stunned by the news I was glad. Sister Lioba's faith in me had proved false; everything about St. Paul's turned out wrong and I did not want to face her. After a year of getting in and out of trouble with the hard-assed Jesuit teachers there, my scholarship was not renewed, and for grade ten I joined my friends at St. John's.

When I graduated under the wrong saint's logo a couple of years later, I discovered something interesting about Sister Lioba. She'd left the convent, quit her order, and married her childhood sweetheart. The big news came from my old buddy Slezak, who had got on the CPR without bothering to finish high school and been transferred to Hamilton. Back in town on holiday in summer, he told me importantly how he worked at the ticket counter, made big bucks and had great benefits, and how, one busy afternoon, he'd bumped into our former teacher, my secret love. She and her husband were living on a farm somewhere on the Niagara peninsula, growing apples; they were expecting their second child.

The really odd thing was that Slezak said he hardly recognized "Ingrid" (no longer "Lioba," of course) when he sold her the ticket—because she had, in his words, "gotten rather fat."

Click

I always knew I was different, not a regular Canadian kid, but an immigrant, a foreigner, emerging from a different cultural background and with a different language at the forefront of my brain; but it was only in high school, in the late sixties, that I began to confront this issue of identity. That's when I started thinking about what it really meant to be ethnic.

Back then, every day at high noon, my grade ten classmates whipped out Saran-wrapped sandwiches, pale bologna beauties, beige on white bread, smudge of bright yellow French's mustard round the edges, pale iceberg lettuce modestly peeking out. They held them high in the lunchroom, little flags proclaiming their connectedness to each other in the realm of a wholesome and progressive Canada.

Everyone had bologna in their sandwiches; that's what made it special. I could smell it, that delicate aroma of mildly smoked meat, gentle, faintly sugary. Everyone ate it, their birthright. Everyone except me. My dark, garlic-stinky kielbasa on caraway rye, hiding its shame in filmy wax paper instead of clear plastic, marked me alien, the outsider.

A new neighbourhood in Winnipeg, a new school, and I wasn't adjusting well—not because I wasn't trying, but because reality kept shifting. One minute everything was readable, signs and signifiers all lined up. Then, in a blink, all was mystery. My ESL background was blocking me from real Canadian life. Written "bologna" but pronounced "baloney"? Why? How did that ba sound get in there? Where did the g in the word go? And how did that ee get in at the end? It was a mystery. Or was it was like the shibboleth story in the Bible that demonstrated you either knew the language or you didn't, the right thing to say. That's what made you part of the tribe.

Fitting in was my desperate goal. Step by precarious step I was trying to find my way into Canadianhood. But I was a refugee who had learned English on his own, the son of fatalistic Poles with a catastrophic history, survivors of war here not by choice but by chance. After being demobbed in England, they were cut off from their corner of the Homeland by the Stalinist regime, and given the option of migrating. Argentina, Australia, New Zealand, Africa, or Canada? They wound up on the Prairies, in Manitoba, because a distant uncle on my mother's side offered encouraging words from the vast empty epicentre of North America. They came, found themselves in a place much like the Siberia they had sought to escape at one point in their adventures, quickly yet bitterly fell out with their new-found relatives, then spent years unhappily struggling for a toehold in Winnipeg's North End. So instead of getting hip to the tango or surfboarding, I failed to master skating on frozen toes. The vicissitudes of the displaced? Maybe just poor coordination. But it didn't help that my parents' house was where the heart was not; their true home was back there in an unknown ancient country across the ocean. So while my address was in the Peg, the place where I ate my pyrogies and changed my socks, our home's psychic core lay on the other side of the planet.

Maybe if my parents had gone back to post-war Poland, experienced again what they'd lost—or thought they had—things might have been different. As it was, my father refused to go anywhere. He never traveled after the long journey of his displacement, determined to stay home where he was safe. My mother tried to visit Poland often in the sixties and seventies, but was always refused; perhaps her name was on some kind of list. We'll never know. At any rate, our house remained a repository of Polish lost causes in which the factors that determined the fate of that country were arduously re-examined daily, while Chopin études tinkled suicidally on the radio in the background.

Each time I opened the front door, entering or leaving, everything changed. Just like that. Coming home from school each day, I stepped into a different country, a place where English was forbidden. Our family talk was Polish—always charged with emotion, full of poetic cadences and weepy rhythms—plus bits of Ukrainian, Russian, German floating in the supercharged air, depending on who was visiting. The languages varied but English was never one of them and the topic was always the same: the war (there was only one, WW II). On and on, endless talk about murky alliances, momentous battles, muddled agendas—a crazy-quilt discourse about history, Hitler, Sikorski (did the Allies assassinate him in that plane crash to appease Russia?), God, massacres, the End of the World. Babel. Chaos.

The decor of my parents' house was apocalyptic, a perfect backdrop to the crazy atmosphere it contained. Aside from a Gainsborough print that had somehow strayed into the house, portraying a serenely beautiful Lady Whatever in cool purples and greys, our home's colour scheme was lurid, a combination of hellish reds and yellows. Living room walls sported Byzantine icons, crucifixes made of hundreds of glued burnt matchsticks, images of haloed popes, a copy of the

Shroud of Turin, a glistering beaten copper Last Supper, and a sheaf of dried Easter wheat. Between them were sprinkled white and vari-coloured doilies in geometric, mostly Russian patterns protecting the furniture. A giant glass bowl of ornately carved, brilliantly painted wood pysanky (Easter eggs) stood on the sideboard. Spoils were scattered here and there: photos of comrades grinning in front of the Pyramids, a silver spoon snatched from Mussolini's palace just hours after he was executed (both my parents, a corporal and an army nurse, were posted nearby), coins from a dozen European countries, shiny bullets—as if universal soldiers had just come in, emptied blood-spattered pockets on every surface. Everywhere you looked, war things and a riot of patterns, colours, symbols.

When I stepped *out* of my parents' house, Canadian life appeared sweetly straightforward. Click, like switching channels: out here two languages, English and French; two kinds of cheese, yellow and white; two kinds of bread, white and brown; two TV stations, come to think of it, that broadcast in unambiguous black and white. It was obvious that's how life should be: a binary system, this/that, one or the other, not all mixed up.

Naturally I hungered, not for the daily Euro-fare of borscht, *golemki* (cabbage rolls), potatoes prepped in dozens of ways, and assorted smoked meats, but for ideologically pure bologna and what it stood for. There it lay in sanctuary behind the cool glass of Safeway's sparkling clean meat counter, next to "skinless" wienies (a miracle?) and shimmering emerald-green Jell-O salads. Row upon row of round slices—oh-so-perfect circles—that cried out continuity, completion, wholeness. Ethereal sausage, processed to a purity of colourless form that rendered its protein origins a sacred mystery. Bologna/baloney: the meatoid of the gods in sacred hosts always there, ready to feed the hungry Canadian multitude, body and soul.

But not me. On my way to school in the morning, I carried the sandwich of doom in my lunchbag, dark smelly food that would betray me to my classmates. Shamefully, I sometimes ditched the lunch my mother carefully made me, bought a camouflaging hot dog from the cafeteria. But I wouldn't throw my lunch away. Couldn't. Brought up on a steady diet of war stories in which the sanctity of food played a crucial role, I knew waste was the worst sin. So I'd drop the brown paper bag into a mailbox at the corner. That way there was a chance food would not be lost. My fantasy was that a hungry mailman would find it. Sure, he'd think it bizarre, but he might be a secret ethnic like me; it could be a sign to him, the smell of kielbasa an unexpected pan-Slavic greeting.

Back home, my attempts at cross-cultural integration bridged no gaps.

"Why don't we ever have any bologna?" I asked one day, hunkered down at the kitchen table over a plate of potato pancakes.

My father snorted. "What for? That junk will kill you."

"For lunch," I said, standing my ground.

"It's not real meat," he declared. "It's ah...pink rubber, garbage, I don't know. It's baloney." He emphasized the ee ending and laughed.

"Don't be silly. There's lots of *good* cold cuts in the fridge," my mother offered. "Ham, beef. Or headcheese, Rysz, delicious this time, believe me!"

They didn't understand me! In the delis of Winnipeg's famously ethnic North End, all was the darkness of flesh and blood, partaking of the atavistic, abbatoirian realm of Old World necessity: glistening red and white sausage in slippery pig-gut casings, golden smoky hams from famous towns, foreboding black puddings—all striated with lines of fat and the variegated hues of animal muscle. Not so with sacred processed New Order sausage; it did not betray primitive carnal roots. From long observation and a few secretly shared bites I knew that bologna was no colour at all, light and tender, soft and fresh tasting, every slice exactly the same, never chewy or smelly and certainly not *meaty*. Whatever special relation it had to a place in Italy had been blessedly lost in the sea change of trans-Atlantic acculturation long ago.

It was so obvious. Then and now, old and new—*of course* the future was what I craved, not a dead past of war and fading culture, but an exquisite ideal of Newness in a world untrammelled by a thousand generations who had lived and died in the muck of history.

For the same reasons I longed for non-Polish friends in the new neighbourhood, to help me learn things Canadian. I used to spend the evenings getting out of the house as much as possible, going to the library on the pretext of school research assignments, hanging out in coffee shops and poolhalls. That's how I met Pat O'Brien and discovered a passion for snooker and the places it was played. Usually you came down a flight of stairs onto a lower floor where the tables were, saw that sea of green baize in a haze of cigarette smoke, dotted with brilliant colours—red, blue, yellow—like an exotic atoll out of the technicolour film version of *South Pacific* suddenly manifest in our bleak prairie-scape. You could hear the click of ball hitting ball every second.

Soon we were skipping school regularly, shooting just for fun, not bets, at Gibson's downtown, hanging out over cups of stale diner coffee afterwards. On some of those drifting days he brought me to his parents' home for supper. Their household included his mom and dad, Pat's brothers Dan and Mike, his sister Eileen, Grandpa, and Bingo the dog. It was with this family that I first saw *Hockey Night in Canada* and also had my first traditional Thanksgiving (a holiday not on the official European list of feast days). Dinner was great, like TV: roast turkey and stuffing, yams and sweet potatoes (vegetables I'd never eaten), peas and cubed carrots, stiff tubular Ocean Spray cranberry sauce, and, for dessert, RediWhipped pumpkin pie with coffee—the very staff of New World family life, stuff I'd only read about, or seen on shows like *Bonanza* or *Father Knows Best.* Our friendship persisted and the family included me on other occasions, like birthdays, for celebratory meals of prime rib with Yorkshire pudding. To start a festive evening, the family played games like cribbage, instead of discussing sucking wounds or political treacheries of the past, and drank Scotch and sodas, gin and tonics, or sherry, never strong, neat water-clear *wodka*, the all-purpose beverage at my home.

Through Pat's sister I met Pamela, a peaches-and-cream high school dream girl one year older than me. She was all blonde hair and blonde legs, framed by long square-cut bangs and micro-miniskirts. But despite her mod Carnaby Street look, Pam was old-fashioned. Right off she invited me to meet her parents. We had an English-style tea that cold afternoon in September: orange pekoe tea with soft white sandwiches—cucumber, egg salad, salmon—jellies on the side, *sweet* pickles, and some mysteriously bland yet curiously satisfying pound cake.

Our love progressed, sort of. Soon Pam was inviting me over every Friday night when her parents went out to the British Legion Hall. Her folks would greet me warmly, then depart, leaving Pam to set the scene; to begin, some medium petting on the couch, then dinner: broiled T-bone steak, served with genuine HP Sauce; Kraft Dinner, with a gourmet touch of bacon and tomato topping; lamb chops with canned peas and Safeway brand mint jelly. Then back to the couch, but for TV watching or listening to records.

After the musical interlude, around 11:00, I'd say good night. A final grope at the door, then out into the cold, trudging eight blocks home in heavy boots, parka, and mitts, lost in a white/black winterland of snow and sky—with a full stomach and the smell of Love's Baby Soft in my nostrils.

Our weird Friday night domesticity—what was with that? Why not necking *after* dinner instead of only before? Truth is I didn't know what "the plan" was. Maybe this was the all-Canadian way of teenage romance. At any rate, I cautiously followed Pam's lead, and these food-structured evenings continued through the winter and into stark prairie spring. Part of it may have been simply logistics. Neither of us had a car and no place to be on our own, so we "played house" whenever the opportunity presented itself. When we did go out, Saturday nights, it was double dating to a movie. In a way I welcomed publicness, the definition and separation of stiff chairs and immovable armrests in the cinema; at Pam's house I *sensed* boundaries and expectations, but could not interpret them, while at the movies the set-up was clear...and the flow of long-desired foods unchecked. The four of us always stopped beforehand for pizza or fish and chips, consumed popcorn throughout the feature, then had coconut or Boston cream pie (but it's *not* a pie, my foreign soul silently cried out), with coffee, afterwards.

Over pie on one such movie night, our double date partners casually mentioned that they were getting married the next week. We were in high school and this seemed a bad idea, but the girls both seemed happy and excited about the news. The soon-to-be-groom, Roger, looked at me wordlessly as if sending a message over the high-pitched feminine chatter that now filled our booth. I wasn't sure what it meant, but Pam and I broke up shortly after the wedding.

Still, I was learning, and every day brought new and better understanding of Canadiana. Dating and hanging out offered chances for food sleuthing and important linguistic insights—exotica banned in my mother's kitchen, like tuna surprise casserole (*surprise*, those are potato chips on top!), meatloaf, shepherd's pie, clam chowder, clubhouse sandwiches, Salisbury steak, etc., was cadged or offered in other, more Canadian homes and local diners. These foodstuffs were more than merely forbidden fruit; they seemed to whisper the dreams of a nation, made up a language that transmitted cultural value, the norms and expectations of a society. I savoured the aristocracy of a shopping cart that cradled "baron of beef," "sirloin," "crown roast." Soon I recognized the ranks of meaty privilege in phrases like "bringing home the bacon" and "living high off the hog." And in idle moments I considered the Freudian slippage of food itself in relation to other appetites: "what a dish," "hot tomato," "cherry," "top banana." My trove of arcana, gleaned from table talk, grew daily. Pound cake was called that because it combined a pound of each ingredient, I heard. Yorkshire puddings were originally cooked beneath the roast to sop up drippings, served before the main course to take the edge off appetite. Cool.

As I penetrated the culture my social life grew. Soon I was going on dates to midnight drive-ins and parties where we writhed to Hendrix while ingesting chip n' dip, Cheezies, pop, illicit beer. There were weekend wienie roasts and barbecues in the summer, and, in the winter, tobogganing excursions; I was doing it all, all year round.

One of the people I met in this social whirl was Darren. His background was Slavic, like mine, but you couldn't tell; he'd shed it long ago, like an outgrown Cossack shirt from a forgotten Folklorama. (What kind of name was "Darren," anyway?) He claimed to speak only English. A tall, lanky fellow who seemed to know everyone, he had an ironic manner and easy grace—sophistication.

Darren lived across the street from school. One day, to my delight, he invited me home for lunch. To start, he opened something called Klik, a small rectangular can with round edges that yielded a seamless lump of pale processed meat, exquisitely bologna-like. Then he toasted Wonderbread, spreading it with French's mustard (no butter). We washed down our "Klikwiches," as Darren called them, with Coke. The combination was terrific: warm toast enclosing a bland yet piquant filling oddly well-matched to the sweet bubbly pop. We ate in the rec room, lounging in La-Z-Boy chairs on one side of a ping-pong table, in front of wall-mounted stereo speakers that framed the TV set and blared Duane Eddy.

I had an insight, my own private bologna epiphany. *This* was what it meant to be Canadian, right here in the mythic rec room, "recreational room," that is, wherein fun and games were to be had, unlike my parents' cement-grey bunker-like basement devoted to orderly racks of home-jarred produce, row upon row, waiting to ward off starvation in the long winter to come. Sitting there, listening to twangy guitar music, Klik n' Coke in hand, I felt the perfect fit. Everything clicked together in a transcendent moment of harmony. I saw that all would turn out right, saw myself moving through life confidently into a shining tomorrow. Unexpectedly, blessedly, I had found the path to true happiness—nothing would harm me in the glorious future.

I decided to promote my mystical insight to the family. The next afternoon I did the shopping, and with the groceries brought home a can of KLIK, a loaf of Wonder Bread, a bottle of French's, a 24-ouncer of Coke.

My parents were putting out lunch on the kitchen table: the usual black bread, liver sausage, headcheese, pickled onions and dills.

"Try something new for a change, Dad." I waved the Klik under his nose, pulled off the attached key and hooked it on the unwinding metal strip that opened the can. The vacuum broke with a fragrant pop, revealing quivering pinkness within.

"New?" he scoffed, pointing to my gift. "That's Spam; we got that in the Army. When there was nothing else to eat—that's what it tastes like. Nothing! Can't you tell what's good? My god! What's wrong with you?"

My mother laughed. "Oh, Frank, let him have it—then he'll know how bad things really were during the War."

"Very funny," I said. With dignity I started toasting the bread, making myself a Klikwich.

"If you like it, eat it," she said philosophically.

And I did, on my own, at the end of the table in solitary splendour.

Ten years later I was on the west coast, in a new life, at grad school with new friends and not much contact with the family. After high school, life on the prairies felt too elemental—the steady sunlight throwing everything into ironic relief, the stark landscape framing human endeavour as if through the wrong end of a telescope on a pygmy scale. I felt observed there, self-conscious, unprivate—everyone knew me, my sordid history and crazy family. Yet, of course, no one *really* knew me. Vancouver, I thought, was so much more my style, all soft, misty and free-flowing. And I was utterly unknown there, free to be, or become my true self. But it had been a bad winter in Lotus Land. Icy rain dripped endlessly from a leaden sky and a serious illness took me in and out of the hospital repeatedly. My mother knew I was sick, of course, and one day a care package arrived. To my surprise, along with the usual Polish goodies was a box of Klik, twenty-four little cans. A joke, maybe, or just a maternal kindness?

I'd never noticed Klik on the store shelves in Vancouver, had forgotten it long before.

Curious, I opened a tin; the metal seal snapped with a happy sound and I smelled the familiar sweetness that brought memories with it. Where was Pam? I wondered. I'd lost sight of her, Pat, the others; they were fuzzed over in my mind like an old movie about high school.

But I still knew the Klik ritual. Of course, adjustments had to be made: instead of Wonder Bread I had sourdough. In place of French's, grainy Pommery mustard, and red wine instead of Coke. The finished product, though, looked as I recalled, golden and inviting. For a moment I hesitated, Klikwich in hand, remembering. Then I took a bite.

The first mouthful was a shock. Bland, mushy, flavourless, barium meal made flesh. I tried again, but it was no use. Nothing was as I remembered it. My well-crafted identity itself was gone. "Pink rubber"—prophetic words of my father—filled my mouth, choking me.

As I sat there chewing on my moment of truth, sick, still feverish, suddenly I knew many things. That Klik *was* second-rate Spam, a humiliating fact that mocked my youthful passion for self-definition. That food itself is conformity, and, then as now, I conformed with gusto to the habits of proto-peers. That what it meant to be Canadian had changed significantly over a generation. And that, in the end, you are what you eat.

My head ached. My throat was sore. But I kept forcing the tasteless sandwich down. Then, on the penultimate painful swallow, it clicked; like my parents before me, and everyone eventually, I had begun to consume my past.

After that penitential sandwich, I began to do it on purpose, trying to reconnect to the *real* ethnic me. Not having thought much about my Euro-heritage in the intervening years, I looked for modest ways to reclaim it. I started celebrating Christmas with some remembered Polish flourishes, sometimes entertained with traditional foods and drinks. I tracked down a recipe for *piluski*, "little fingers" of potato dumpling, the Polish answer to gnocchi, I guess, and learned to make a mean *bigos* (a hunter's stew we used to have back home). I began to keep Wyborowa *wodka* in the freezer, purchased *kalishki* (tiny glasses) to sip it from properly, like wine. Later still, I returned to the original spelling of my first name, Ryszard. At the same time I was surprised to discover, when revisiting the Peg and seeing childhood friends, that quite a few had changed their names or, long divorced, clung to acquired married monikers (Smith, Jones, Adams) to disguise their origins, to fit in. First names were dumped too: Danutas were now Donnas, Bogdans truncated to Dans—as if they were traveling in the opposite direction of me.

Around this time, however, I also started to recognize a deep ambiguity in my sense of cultural identity. Why had I never traveled to Poland? My one attempt many years back to attend the Jagiellion Institute in Cracow was derailed by that illness in grad school, but once I'd recovered I never made another attempt to go. Likewise I didn't attend artistic or cultural events related to anything Polish. Nor could I claim to practise my first language anymore, on purpose or even via happenstance. It had been years since I'd taken a Polish course or tried to read anything substantial in the language; when I did try to figure out something short, it was often baffling. If I was standing in line someplace and people in front of me started chatting in Polish, I'd remain silent. And so on…less and less was I linguistically connected to my roots.

Normally I don't think about these distancing mechanisms. When I do, I tell myself that it has something to do with things I hate about my heritage, that—though engendered in the long-ago—certain themes still have nasty currency. Class-consciousness is one such atavism, derived from a legacy of petty (really petty) aristocracy that was the largest in all of Europe. Then there is the inescapable fact of a history of brutal anti-Semitism in Poland, along with a staunch Catholicism wherein something like 98% of the population until recently belonged to the one true Xian Church. Such Old World associations make it ugly to be part of the New.

But maybe it's a lot more personal, rooted in my own weird, divided psychology. Maybe the truth is I don't exactly feel Polish or Canadian, but simply Other. I noticed this curious dissonance a few years ago on my first trip to France. Right away I felt at home there, like it was correct to be an alien. On the other hand, perhaps I was just following the ghosts of all those Polish émigrés (Mickiewicz, Slowacki, Chopin, and lots of lesser knowns); Poles have always looked to Paris as the summit of art and the good life, lived there in droves, so maybe my sense of connection was not so strange, so Other really.

Unlike me, my partner is fluent in French and had managed all our daily interactions on the trip while I dumbly attended in the background. It was odd yet pleasurable to shed responsibilities, power, and linguistic skin in this detached way; I felt nurtured by all of France, enclosed in shared experience and non-verbal communion, caressed by every gesture, each moment of eye contact. When I eventually ventured out alone, I pushed the language envelope further, pretended to be Polish with the French shopkeepers, babbling a few words in my first language. There I'd stand in warm sunlight, like an idiot or a mime, grinning, pointing with one hand while displaying shiny francs in the other. Perhaps they understood me less than if I'd tried to speak English or guidebook French, yet they were always warm, respectful of my alienness, and carefully precise in making exact change.

To me there was a liberation in *not* speaking, a shock of freedom I still can't really explain. Sure there's a "cool web of language" that binds us together—gives meaning to our daily actions, makes us whole by creating continuity. Yet is it, as the poem suggests, also a trap, shutting us off from some fundamental aspect of self that exists on a more primitive level?

Something that happened just before returning to Canada makes me think so. We had left lovely Lyon to return to Paris on the TGV for a few final days before flying to Vancouver. By then we were traveling with my partner's mother, who had joined us in the south. They were speaking

English, exclaiming at the blurred beauty of the wine country outside the windows, settling plans for our time in the City of Light, and so on. Having trouble making out their words over the surrounding, competing babble, and feeling very sad to be leaving France, I naturally decided to go to the bar car.

The train was full of high school students, so packed you had to step over them on the floor. As I made my way barward I spotted someone's folded newspaper, realized this was the last day of the *Tour de France* and that everyone was going to Paris for the finale.

After a quick drink I headed back to my seat. As I negotiated my way around more chattering, jostling kids on the floor of a passageway between cars, the train slowed, stopped. Suddenly doors slid open next to me. People jumped in, others exited; in the bustle I got turned round, pushed out onto the station landing of a tiny village surrounded by vineyards.

For a moment everything froze, and I had a fleeting but full vision of *not* getting back on the TGV, of a whole new life: myself quietly waiting for the train to start up, then walking down the tracks, burying my wallet under a tree, making myself out to be a deaf-mute, gaining simple work picking grapes—and never talking again. I'd be safe, lovable, my true new-found self existing in a cocoon of silence, my body speaking warmly for me.

The vision lasted one ringing moment, like when you feel the world is about to shift irrecoverably. Then as the TGV hissed, I jumped back on, of course, and the doors clicked shut behind me.

COEUR DU BOIS

Another Labour Day. Back to school, the end of summer and of freedom—a death sentence. Ahead was a calendar full of classes and an unfathomable wasteland of the future. We were trapped and there was no escape. Some revelation, upheaval, change needed to happen.

And then something did.

Like every fall, the change of season was starting to shorten the days and brighten the colours of the trees, as if calling out for dramatic action: without *and* within. My friend Roger and I spent most of it driving in and around the edges of town and beyond for hours in his red MG, on and off the Perimeter Highway, looking for I'm not sure what—a discovery?

"Think I'll try this road," he said.

"Doesn't look very promising, Rog," I said. It was rutted, grown over with weeds, as if seldom used.

But he was, as always, romantic: "Maybe we'll find something..."

That was true year round, of course, what I remember most about being a teenager, a feeling of being suspended between stagnation and anticipation. Like most of us in our latter teens, my buddies and I had a lot of energy but no purpose. That's when some of us first got cars, and so we'd roam all day, all night sometimes, driving and driving, circumnavigating the city—too quickly because of Winnipeg's smallness—and loitering in its familiar districts seeking distractions that just weren't there, until we got so tired and bored that the only thing left was sleep. On our meandering journeys all the roads we traveled turned into dead ends, and so, eventually, we would retrace our steps and head home, defeated. Occasionally we would wind up at the airport for coffee, late at night, comforted by the sense of other people escaping, moving through time and space, going someplace.

A couple of times we just jumped in and kept going in a straight line, once to Calgary without even telling our parents, coming back a couple of days later when the money ran out. Then, that same year, in a somewhat more organized way, we headed north to Churchill, just to see the northernmost town in Manitoba, get the T-shirt, but got so dispirited by the increasingly bleak landscape that we turned back only a few miles from our destination. Driving was the thing, I guess, that illusory sense of movement that it provided—as if we had a destination, something to do; or perhaps, at a less conscious level, we were searching for an activity that would somehow redeem or transform us.

Unlike my other friends, Roger always had a car. He had dropped out of high school and got a job at sixteen, working in a low-end garage part-time, doing oil changes and minor servicing; so he had real money, plus access to and knowledge about cars. A year or so after he first obtained a driver's licence, he got "shot-gunned." We had double dated, and his girlfriend from one of those evenings became pregnant.

That's when Roger found a more serious job as an IBM typewriter repairman, rented a nice oak-floored apartment with a fireplace on old-fashioned Wolseley Avenue near the river, and, in some ways, started his own life.

What originally brought us together as friends was a shared sense of trappedness, especially on the home and family front, even though he was much more Canadian than me. He'd been born here, had always spoken English, and so on. But, like mine, Roger's parents were difficult, though in his case it might be more accurate to say eccentric. His father, Ivan, was already old, sixty-six, when Roger was fifteen. Ivan, a kind and truly gentle man, had "retired" at thirty-nine after a health scare which turned him into a lifelong vitamin fanatic. Roger's mom, Agnes, was a psychic, a true gypsy with French bloodlines, and bright sparkling eyes that mesmerized you. Not only did she read tea leaves, cards, and palms for cash in a local restaurant, she lived and breathed the spirit world of Madame Blavatsky and her gang, Ouspensky, all theosophic stuff, and, more generally, a parallel universe of unseen reality that impinged on ours. "Mrs. Christie," as I always thought of her, even when I was old enough to use her first name—maybe because the name sounded so ironically normal—never stopped "reading"the shadow world. It used to drive Roger nuts that she would call him at work ten, twenty times a day, using her occult powers to catch him in whatever office he was at, servicing IBM typewriters and charming secretaries, because she had seen in a vision that his car was about to be ticketed for a parking infraction, or some other looming domestic catastrophe, like birds getting caught in the chimney of his apartment. What bothered him was not so much the interference but that she was invariably right; he regularly received five to ten tickets a month, at the times and places she predicted, but denied it when his mother asked.

About the birds in the chimney I don't know. All I do know is that while I did not believe in fortune telling and the psychic lifestyle, many times she demonstrated her sibylline power to me personally and those around me. One time, for example, over at my parents' for tea, Mrs. Christie embarrassed my mother hugely by revealing that she—my mother, that is—had recently purchased a costly string of pearls for herself. It was true, though my mother had never told any of us. Flushing red, overcome by the supernatural authority of Mrs. Christie's bland, smiling words, my mother went to her bedroom and came back to shamefacedly show us her hidden jewels.

With his other-worldly mom and a vitamin-obsessed dad, maybe it's not surprising that at home, there was never any decent food for Roger, only chaos, mystery, and cabbalistic speculations. Ivan seemed far too busy with his fruit juicing and hundreds of interacting self-medications to notice that his wife did not really cook, shop, clean, or keep house like a normal 1950s mom. One day, I remember, Roger and I stopped in at his parents' house in the late afternoon. Atypically, Ivan was dining in the kitchen, enjoying what he said was "a really tasty stew." We were dubious, but said nothing. Turned out it was a pot of bones and offal that Mrs. Christie was rendering to feed their dogs. I don't know if Ivan ever found out, or if it would have mattered.

She was truly uncanny, constantly experiencing phenomena and articulating her revelations in a convulsive, obsessed way to anyone who would listen (reminding me of my mother, of course, and her endless horror-soaked war stories that she would insistently detail to complete strangers, on the bus, in the check-out line at Safeway). Ivan, meanwhile, inhabited his own private planet, light years from Mrs. Christie's, keeping mostly to his room where he rested healthfully, napping through much of the day so that he could be up at night meticulously taking his dozens of different vitamin and herb supplements on a carefully timed schedule.

Meanwhile at my parents' place, despite a different set of problematic psychic parameters, there was always decent food, and lots of it after the lean first years. Roger often showed up at dinnertime, and was warmly welcomed by my mother, who always loved to feed anyone, friend or stranger. Afterwards, though, we had to get out, go away, hit the road, drive on and on, looking for adventure. For both of us, home was a madhouse, while our nine-to-five realities—school and jobs—seemed to be leading nowhere. We had nothing exciting to do and no specific place we wanted to go. Life was vague and aimless.

When Roger got married, I expected that the routine of him and me cruising around endlessly on weekends, and after and during work/school (we both played hookey often) would end, but in a way it didn't. Roger took on the breadwinner role, switching from part-time gas pumping to full-time typewriter repairs without much problem, but he had little interest in the duties of being a husband and, quickly thereafter, a father, at least to my eye. Maybe marriage felt like just another kind of trap. But we still hung out and goofed around like unfettered teens while Roger's wife was stranded at home—and strangely, though I had always liked Roger's girlfriend, I hardly thought of this apparent unfairness as we extended our roaming further and further afield and for longer and longer periods.

For the short time of the honeymoon Roger was not available. But then things got back to normal. For the true romance of roaming and driving adventures, you couldn't beat Roger. On that particular Labour Day, for instance, he was persistent. We went down the neglected, weedy road, and by accident found what we called *Coeur du Bois*, in honour of Roger's partial Frenchness, thinking of the Québécois runners in the woods, the *coureurs de bois*, but getting it mixed up with some kind of "wood heart," which actually turned out not to be so inappropriate. We had parked where the road stopped, and stumbled on it when we were trying to find a way to the river, planning to sit on the bank and drink beer. There was a bit of a pathway, and we trekked a few hundred yards through scrubby woods, six-packs of Molson beer growing heavy under our arms. The sun was getting low, and you could smell autumn on the cooling air.

We wound up in a barren ravine surrounded and canopied by tall deciduous trees. It was a perfect sheltered secret spot, a declivity of about 40 x 20 feet that cut off the endless prairie wind, a few feet from the river, a warm bower of black dry earth with a small pile of burned-out charcoaled branches and cinders from previous fires at its centre.

Who knows how many fires had burnt here? It felt ancient, like the slow beating heart of the woods. We imagined French Canadian explorers and trappers coming downriver and stopping at this perfect haven to build a fire, roast some just-shot meat, and nestle down for the night.

The river was only a few feet away and made a gentle sound in the background, although you actually didn't see it because of the trees at its edge. We sat down on a quilt of dry leaves that covered most of the ground around the bare fire pit. It smelled warm and dry, like familiar old wool blankets. As the evening cooled, we decided to build a fire, hearkening to the cavelike mood of the place, a primitive sense of safe enclosure, the *coeur*. We collected a couple of armfuls of fallen branches and twigs, tore up the beer box for kindling. The wood caught perfectly first time.

So we sat talking, drinking. After another beer we noticed the sky was dark. Then the fire flared up, some of the burnt wood we had built it on catching flame beneath in a burst. The bonfire cast weird shadows onto the trees around and over our heads, and on us, faces flickering, our clothes glowing red.

I don't know who did the first jump, Roger or I. Somehow we both wound up running down the long sloping expanse of the ravine, and leaping over the flame—laughing, yelling, breathless from the beer and physical effort, flying through the air across the cusp of the gully, warmed by the licks of fire, landing hard on the other side. Then having another beer. And running again, like kids or cavemen, letting go, fire jumping in the night.

We came back a few days later, with more guys, including Ken, Roger's distant relation, a cousin. At fourteen he had fallen hopelessly in love with a girl in his high school, and, when things ended badly, tried to blow his head off. But he did it lying on his back in bed, sticking a rifle into his mouth, and when he pulled the trigger, the bullet blew off most of his upper lip and all of his nose. Somehow, this did no life-threatening damage. Years later his face was still dramatically deformed, enough to make strangers stare.

As darkness fell, though, Ken didn't look that much different from the rest of us in the flickering light from the bonfire, Roger and me and the others we started to bring along as autumn took hold of the countryside. The guys we knew, all of us, were young, tense, rudderless. Maybe, really, we were all freaks, one way or another, all running from something, hiding some malformation or oddity, some ugliness in our daylit regular lives. Soon about a dozen of us became regulars, planning to meet out at *coeur du bois*, the magic heart beating deep in the forest.

It was always the same routine: the beer, the fire, the meandering talk—and then the moment when suddenly someone would do the first jump, followed by another and another until, fueled by the beer, urged on by the settling cold blackness of night, of winter, oncoming, we found the unexpected perfect arc, the momentary release, flying through icy air into the eternal light of the fire.

WHO DO YOU LOVE?

The year I turned seventeen, Winnipeg's summer was unusually hot and sultry from June to September. Old people complained and tried to sit outside evenings despite the mosquitoes; young people loved it, the warm nights of minimally clothed hanging out, partying, and cruising around in the soft air—unless they were working, that is. I had a job that summer at the Grey Goose Bus Lines garage on Burnell Street, off Portage, arranged by my father who had worked there many years as late-night supervisor. My shift started at 4:00 p.m. and went to midnight, or later, because most of the buses came in at the end of the day, and the charters were unpredictable. Sometimes I'd be lucky to catch the last city bus back to the North End at 1:30 a.m.

It was a lousy job, in a way. After long-haul trips under a blistering prairie sky, over hundreds of miles and without air conditioning, the heat from the big motors and sun-drenched metal turned those old buses into ovens, despite wide-open windows. Once the buses were finally parked for the night by my dad, an art in itself, thanks to the tight spacing of the garage, my main task was to swab them out with bucket and mop, sloshing the linoleum down the centre aisle and under the seats, readying them for their next rendezvous with fun. By the time I got on, mop in one hand, heavy bucket of steaming sudsy water in the other, and walked to the back of the bus where I'd start my actual washing work, I'd already be drenched, sweat running down my face, my open shirt a wet rag.

On the other hand, it was a great job because I made money. And there was an added bonus; you found all sorts of things on the buses, especially the charters that really ran as booze-soaked junkets. People forgot or lost things, and rarely followed up to make a claim. As they reclined or snoozed, stuff slid out of their polyester pockets and plastic purses, cash that wound up on the floor or stuck between the seats, and other things: plush toys, slippery shrink-wrapped single condoms, almost untouched lipsticks, hotel keys, partial cartons of duty-free Lucky Strikes and Marlboros. Often there was booze, too, bourbon and American beer left behind. Once I found $55 in a plain chrome money clip, pretty big bucks in those days.

For me it was a kind of Monday-to-Friday archaeological dig, the buses from those faraway "exotic" places—Fort Frances, Minot, Reno—offering up vicarious mementos of trips to realms of adult pleasureland, where there was gambling, liquor, sex, all the good things of life my teenage money could not yet buy, at least not legally.

On weekends, though, when I was off work, things were pretty tame for me. Sure there were visions of cool parties that might be happening, places where you might meet hot girls, become one with the youth culture that was supposedly everywhere in 1967; but basically, like many summers before, I'd be going to the lake to get out of the sweltering city, the concrete-paved North End, with the guys—buddies whose parents, unlike mine, had cottages. We'd been doing this for years, same faces, same poker games, same boys' night out. Same-old same-old, but it was fun. After all, we'd grown up together, shared a lot of history as altar boys and on the softball team that played against other parochial schools. By now the cottage trip was a tradition, a well-established pattern since grade eight, dependable, reassuring, easy. True, as we all entered adulthood, other factors were theoretically on the horizon, like serious girlfriends, the potential of starting real jobs or going on to university, the scary idea of a future, and so on. But this summer it could still work, the buzzed-out all-male marathon card game at the lake.

In fact, unlike most of the other guys, I already had a girlfriend, sort of, Wanda, the Polish Princess. The problem was she had gone off to the Polish language institute in Detroit, where she went every summer to improve her ethnic heritage knowledge or something. All that nationalistic and historical baggage, the stuff I'd for years been trying to forget, she embraced. We'd been through elementary at Holy Ghost together, always in the same classroom, but didn't really connect until she was at St. Mary's High and I was on scholarship at St. Paul's, the Jesuit-run supposedly best high school in town. These single-sex Catholic schools sponsored dances together, for wholesome boy-girl socializing purposes. One night there she was: a girl I almost did not recognize, in a strapless blue party dress with billowing skirt buoyed by stiff petticoats, her swept-back blonde hair glistening like a crown. Vivacious, bright, lively, classy in every Polish way. We danced. Then we dated, in an infrequent, car-less sort of way. Now we were on our second summer as "an item," though what kind was not exactly clear.

I was confused. When we were alone, which was rare, there was occasional mild kissing and groping, but she never seemed that interested, remaining aloof and cool to my awkward come-ons. Yet she was always friendly and would sometimes actually phone *me* to suggest boy-girl outings we could attend together—like she was my girlfriend, all settled. Was she just "saving" herself for marriage, the proper thing, and didn't want things to get unpleasant, or dangerous? No way was I ready to be married (though my best friend, Roger, at sixteen had been in a strange combination of romantic union and shotgun farce). Anyway, we didn't discuss such things, the Princess and I.

Unlike me, Wanda lived on the right side of the tracks, across town in Fort Rouge, a bus trip away, and her parents didn't exactly welcome me with open pan-Slavic arms. They were polite but reserved, vague in their eye contact, and I quickly got the impression that their princess was meant for something far better than a North End kid like me, whose mom was a cleaning lady sometimes and who, unlike their daughter, did not take his Polishness all that seriously.

Not only did Wanda travel every summer to Detroit or Cracow, she was always signing up for extra Polish courses in town, attending Slavic cultural events when they came up, and, overall, appeared to be grooming herself as the embodiment of a *pani*, or Polish "lady." She played the piano, Chopin, of course; made traditional cookies for the bazaars at Holy Ghost Parish, like *chruscik* (deep fried sweet twists sprinkled with confectioner's sugar); sang sweetly in our mother tongue in the choir at Sunday services. A hard-working husband, a gaggle of well-behaved kids, a house in the suburbs, the support of worthy Polish causes, charitable works in general—that's what seemed to hover above Wanda's halo. And she would be perfect for it all.

That first summer she asked me to accompany her to "Celebrating Polish Culture" at the Fort Garry Hotel, a gala affair in September, semi-formal, with an orchestra and dinner and speeches. In a way it was the last thing I would ever want to do, an old people thing—yet I was flattered, and scrounged for a week to buy a black suit and tie. We went, we waltzed, ate chicken Kiev, listened to the Mayor praise the contributions made by Poles to our fair metropolis. It was OK. Next day a photograph of Wanda and me, prominent in a group of looking-sharp Polish youth dancing the night away, appeared on the society page of the local paper; and I had a sinking feeling that we were meant for each other, me and the Princess, that all the Euro craziness that I had been trying to escape at home would rise up and engulf me no matter what I did—and maybe I would be happy when that happened? It was the pattern of domestic bliss my parents most certainly wanted for me, since I was "too much of a Bolshevik," according to my mother, to become a priest: the ideal for so many Catholic first sons. She cut the photo out of the paper, stuck it in her dresser mirror; Wanda would certainly do as a second choice, right after God himself. That was the impression I got. It felt like things were closing in, and I drifted along in my usual passive way, without much of a plan.

The biggest Princess problem, though, was not Wanda's family; it was her best friend, Victoria. She clung to Wanda in a possessive, protective, obsessive manner. On our dates, most times Victoria would be there, too, in front of the movie house when I arrived. Tall and gawky, pale and weirdly dressed, she was always an unwelcome surprise, tagging along like some kind of chaperone, plopping down next to Wanda in the coffee shop booth after the film, giving me funny looks across the table, now and then offering up sarcastic remarks when I said something, putting herself between us.

Not that Wanda cared, apparently. She never warned me, never said, for instance, "Oh, and it looks like Victoria's going to meet us at the movie." And she never complained about the third wheel either, even when Victoria was momentarily not around. It seemed a conspiracy. I'd turn up and find not Wanda but the two of them, meaning that all I could hope for at the end of the evening was a good-night peck on the cheek, not to mention a fairly bland triangulated outing in every way...which seemed to suit Wanda just fine.

One afternoon, while swilling cheap beer at Pete's place with the guys, his folks being away on vacation, and feeling fuddled by yet another threesome date with Wanda and Victoria the night before, I kvetched about this weird girl-buddy dynamic. The guys' wisdom came swiftly:

"She's a lesbo, man," Stan snorted.

"Get real," Pete chimed in. "Check that butch haircut."

"And all through school," Stan added, "nothin' but track suits. Ever see her in an actual dress? Huh? What's that about?"

"Face it. You got competition, Dicky," Pete added. "Gotta show Wanda the *big* difference." He yanked at his crotch and laughed.

"Lesbians?" I said. "You guys been reading too much porno."

There were other things about Victoria, beside the unfeminine clothes and hair, that did not fit. She was not like a real North Ender, being of English background with a faint Brit accent. She lived out of the district and was delivered by her dad mornings at school, from St. James or somewhere. She was also weirdly athletic for a girl, played tennis, volleyball, and rode horses, I'd heard. In fact, *she* was kind of "horsey," in that androgynous Englishy way you saw in films. Could the lesbian explanation be right?

True or not, what I really didn't understand was why Wanda encouraged the relationship. For sure *she* was no lesbian, whatever Victoria might be or feel—after all, Wanda was Polish! I knew that girls had best girlfriends, often homely semi-losers who teamed up with the attractive babes and lived in their shadows. But that was supposed to be a backgrounder to the essential boy-girl road to happiness, something easily shed when things got serious between a he and a she. Those best girlfriends I imagined spiraling down to various kinds of spinsterhood, long-serving waitressing, grade school teaching, and so on.

Finally, during a brief moment of privacy, I asked Wanda: "What's with this Victoria anyway?" She looked nervous, vague: "I think she's...lonely." But I didn't buy it. More like Victoria was on guard duty, protecting the Princess's honour, I thought, keeping me at arm's length at Her Highness's orders.

Whatever it was, Wanda was gone for the whole summer this year so I went to the cottage with the guys often because I was lonely, too, just like Victoria, I guess; and they were reliably there, my old friends. Still I felt unsatisfied, ill done by. Maybe I didn't miss Wanda so much as I did the general company of any girls, whether that included the possibility of romance or not, but my Wanda-status was well known to all (though I did not broadcast the news) and seemed to make it impossible to actually pursue anyone female in my limited social circle.

So I was relegated to hanging out with the guys in an endless swearing, beer-guzzling, card-playing limbo. But I did like that, too, the dopey, dizzy continuity of it, and who would I pursue anyway? Better to enjoy the sodden pleasures of cottage life, especially as it matched up with the path of least resistance, always my preferred route.

Although Ziggy's and Stan's parents had cottages, we usually went to Ron's parents' place. Being rather primitive, it required the least maintenance—no worries about breaking fancy knick-knacks or doing tricky cleanups late Sunday night before heading back to town. Everything, all the furnishings, was broken, cracked and/or stained already, and the cottage's simple layout made it easy to tidy in a few minutes. Besides, it stood empty every summer; Ron's parents could never make time to come out, even though it was only an hour's drive east of town, on the Winnipeg River in the Whiteshell. This was because the Hesslars ran a grocery store in the North End, open six days a week, famous for sausages made by Ron's dad, and they almost never closed. So we could go to the cottage whenever we wanted, without special arrangements, parental permissions or other uncool hassles.

On the August 1st long weekend Ron and I were supposed drive up to meet the others—Ziggy, Pete, and Stan—but this time at Stan's parents' log cabin, a classier place out past Falcon Lake, for what he promised would be a party with "real live girls." We were to rendezvous at the dock around 9:00; the only access to the cabin was by water, and Stan was to pick us up in his dad's restored 1940s speedboat, a mahogany beauty with sleek lines and an inboard engine. Pictures danced in my mind. Like dark figures out of a Bogart flick, we would skim across the lake in the silvery moonlight to the distant shore, where beautiful girls, some of Sharon's (Stan's steady) friends waited. I felt no pang at the contemplation of infidelity to the Princess—it would be Wanda's fault for not being here. If she even cared. This time, I thought, everything would be different, a weekend to remember.

My mission was to get the beer, always the tricky part of any outing for our underaged group, and Ron was to supply the food as usual. His family had taken the grocery-home concept of my childhood to a whole new level. The store they ran was way bigger than any regular corner store, with aisles and aisles of shelved goods plus a meat counter at the back. It was a self-contained, fairly complete mini-supermarket, taking up a whole city house lot. The Hesslars lived in a comfortable, messy house right across from it, thirty feet away door to door; even in winter they'd dash across the intervening space in shirt sleeves and street shoes, braving the ice and snow, then hunker down in front of the TV with whatever whisked-off-the-shelves convenience food from the market took their fancy. Most times, they all, including Ron's sisters' kids, who lived there with her mysterious unemployed French Canadian husband, had very dissimilar meals at widely different times, making for a sort of non-stop buffet feeling in their living room.

That night I ran into Ziggy's flakey and easily corruptible older brother, Stephen, who worked as a waiter on the trains: "Hey, Steve, can you help Zig out? He needs some beer for a party he's throwin' at the cottage."

He grinned. "What's in it for me?"

"Look, we just need four twelve-packs. How about a carton of smokes for your trouble?"

"You got it."

We picked up bribe smokes for Steve and some for us, and the beer at the nearest beer parlour on McPhillips. Then we drove back to the Market, where I stowed the supplies in its station wagon, a white Pontiac with the store's blue sausage logo on the front doors—we were taking it to the lake. I came out of their garage and looked through the Hesslars' living room window, saw the family in closing time mode, sitting around watching *Bewitched*, eating bratwurst and sauerkraut, beans and wienies, chili, burgers, Cheezies, etc., sipping Pepsis. Ron was in there already; he waved me in while explaining to his folks that we were overnighting it at the cottage.

"Take some food, Ronnie—but not expensive things, you *drek*," Mrs. Hesslar offered gruffly without taking her eyes off wholesome, perky Samantha. In her vocabulary I think that meant something akin to "bum," but in an indulgent way.

Inside the store, I asked about the grocery plunder: "Don't they ever notice what's missing?"

"Nah. Nobody keeps inventory, except for the smokes. Here, buckeroo." He handed me an empty cardboard box. "Grab some relish, chips, you know, the usual, while I get some meat—oh, and lots of buns for sure." It was quiet and dark; we did not turn on the lights in case someone from the house spotted how much we were taking. A magical abundance of tinned and packaged goods glinted in the golden light of the setting sun that still streamed through the big front window of Hesslar's Market as I tiptoed through the store. It was all at my fingertips, my grocery-home dream come true: I scooped up tins of Puritan Beef Stew, Klik, Bick's pickle relish, McGavin's buns and bread, French's mustard, Campbell's soups, Heinz Pork n' Beans, Libby's Fruit Cocktail (I really liked the gooseberries), Ripple chips, V8 Juice, Kraft Cheese Slices, instant coffee, cans of 7-Up and Coke, cookies of various brands—everything, without care or thought of expense.

We arrived at the dock right on time, but no boat. We waited. It was a hot and humid night, and we sat in the car, smoking, sweating, sticking to the plastic upholstery, automatically swatting bugs that got in our cigarette-smoke venting/breathing air window slits. It was claustrophobic inside the wagon but too buggy outside, even for a quick pee. The sun sank, and it got ominously pitch black, stifling.

"Bet it's nice on the water," I said, "on the boat."

"Yeah," Ron answered. "Where is that asshole, anyway?"

We drank more warm beer, smoked, cursed Stan, the mosquitoes. Clearly something had gone wrong with the big plan. Around eleven we decided to try to get some sleep. Ron crawled into the flat, folded-down back of the station wagon with the boxes of food and beer, and I huddled in the front seat, with my knees wedged under the steering wheel. The mosquitoes kept getting in. They buzzed our heads; even if they did not bite, the noise made it impossible to sleep. Finally, after an hour or so, we gave up and hit the road to the Hesslar cottage. Forty-five minutes later we turned on the fridge, stored the food, had a few more drinks, and flipped into bed.

In the morning, there was a pounding on the door: the guys.

Stan apologized, "Something wrong with the boat; couldn't pick you up. Sorry about that."

"What about the girls?" I asked. "They out in the car?"

Ziggy snorted. "What girls?"

"Hey, that was Sharon's screw-up. Last minute she couldn't make it—I dunno, that time of the month—and they wouldn't come on their own." Stan sighed.

Ron laughed. "Guess we're still altar boys. You guys set up the card table; I'll make some breakfast..."

We had sausages and eggs, toast, coffee, and then played all day, right through a late lunch of sandwiches. "That's how the sandwich got invented," I told them. "So Lord Sandwich wouldn't have to interrupt his gambling at the table."

"You're shittin' me," John said. "But, then, do I *really* care?"

"Look it up in the *Brittanica*, chucklehead. You can hold it in one hand, right?" I waved my ham and cheese in his face. "Play with the other."

"Ah, play with yourself—deal the fuckin' cards, man."

As we played and drank, my mood darkened steadily. No-show girls, no-go weekend, a bust. After twelve steady hours of poker, it was getting dark; I spotted the rising moon out the front window. This was so nowheresville, I thought, another Saturday night with the guys, drinking, talking dirty.

Big deal. I felt older than this. I thought of Wanda, my semi-girlfriend, due back late August. Maybe things would heat up; though now that I had been thrown out—well, actually, told not to return in the fall to St. Paul's because of a fist fight during chapel period—I wasn't sure how she'd react. Or how her parents would. Then I thought of Victoria, her nasty laugh and long horsey face, always there, waiting in the shadows, and got even more bummed out.

"Hey." I jumped up. "I'm taking a break, going for smokes."

"Whatsamatter, chickenshit?"

"Hurry back, we're gonna clean your clock," Stan yelled as I lurched for the door.

It was a beautiful evening, still balmy, the water glittering under a rising moon. I followed the river down the half mile to the little grocery store that also doubled as the tiny community's gas station, post office, and liquor outlet (selling two kinds of beer and wine, plus some rye, Scotch, and gin). For a moment I thought of just walking to the highway, hitchhiking back to town right then. But most everyone was settled in for the evening, and I might not get a ride. That would suck too. Like everything.

The store was closing up when I got there, the owner surly. Quickly I bought my smokes and headed back to the door. It snapped open in my face, and there was—Victoria.

For a second I did not even recognize her. She was tanned, in short denim shorts and a pretty, well-filled pink tank top, not the pale grumpy girl in a track suit I remembered. Her shapely bare arms, shoulders, and face were golden with a delicate overlay of pink, like she'd been out all day on the water. Her eyes, lake-blue, her hair, longer than before, sparkled. Obviously, *she* was having a great summer.

"Richard." She gave me a big smile. "What—" She noticed the shutting-down activity beyond me. "Wait, just let me grab something." She rushed past me into the store.

"V-Victoria?" I mumbled, and then "shit" under my breath. Now I was stuck. With Victoria. The perfect end to a perfect day.

She picked a loaf of bread off the shelf, paid, and came back up to me. We went out the door. She waved the bag playfully, and a scent of lilacs wafted through the air. Perfume? On Victoria? "Toast, for breakfast. Surprise, to see you here." She laughed happily; the first time, I think, I'd ever heard her laugh naturally. "At the lake."

"River," I corrected idiotically. "With friends, the guys. How about you?"

"Family, the usual. We come every summer. My folks have a cottage. That way." She pointed in the direction of the Hesslar place. We started walking. I was still dazed by the coincidence, that all these summer weekends we might have been only a hundred or so feet apart without knowing it. Though, of course, what difference, since we hated each other? Still, it was weird. It made me blurt: "Actually, I was, uh, thinking about you a little while ago. Well, Wanda and you."

"Really? How is she?"

"Haven't heard much. One letter. Seems OK, in Detroit, at the Institute."

"Oh, right. The Institute. I'd forgotten." Her eyes and teeth shone bright in the darkness.

She'd forgotten? I stared for a moment, thrown off; this was unreal, a dream. Victoria was a minor babe suddenly, and friendly, not my enemy, plus did not seem to care much about Wanda, guard duty, all that. How could she forget her Princess, her best friend? Where was the fealty? What the hell was going on?

Looking for distraction, I glanced up at the sky, started babbling: "Hey, there's Venus, the Evening Star," I pointed. "First one out at night; that's why they call it—"

"Oh, and isn't that Mars to the right, over there?"

"Yeah, how did you know?"

"I remember you talking about it, after we went to see *2001: A Space Odyssey.* Read up on it."

There was a pause. Then she asked, "Will it get redder, later in the night?"

"Whaa"—I slipped on a rock, almost fell.

"Mars," she replied.

"Oh. Sure." Then I remembered, the astronomy/astrology chat over post-movie coffee. "Yeah, Wanda hated that Kubrick film *so much*; guess there was nothing very Polish in it." We laughed disloyally, pleasurably—her arm brushed mine.

And then we were at the cottage, too soon, next to the sausagemobile and John's gleaming black Ford XL coupe. I didn't want it to end, couldn't face going back inside to the boys and abandoning this "real live girl."

"We're a few lots down on the left," Victoria said, rather dreamily. There was a slight pause, then I thought of something I could offer: "Hey, you want to have a smoke? We can sit on the steps."

"I don't smoke—could hang out for a...bit, though. It is a lovely night."

We sat down. But we could hear the guys laughing, cursing each other out. Of course every third word was fuck or cunt. She looked uncomfortable, hearing all the dirty talk, and our conversation seemed to die. I puffed on my cigarette. Splat—she smacked a mosquito on her thigh. Lucky bug, I thought. What a way to go.

"Then you can suck my—" Ziggy shouted. But I spoke over him: "Wanna come in, say hi to the guys?"

"Not really." She smiled. "Especially after hearing all that."

This was not cool. Here was this girl who apparently hated me but now was acting nice and looking good, and I had no idea what to do next to keep her there. Frantically I looked around, what could I suggest? John's black coupe gleamed like water in the moonlight. "Look," I said, "we can...um...sit in the car. If you...Keep away the bugs?"

"OK," she said.

We walked over and I opened the passenger door of John's car, newer, cleaner than the station wagon. It had two huge doors, the way sports coupes did in those days, swivel bucket seats, plus a big back seat. The interior was all in red leather. We got in, she going straight into the back, maybe because the front seat had been left tilted forward. I got in beside her and rolled the window down an inch, flicked the butt of my smoke out. It arced in the sky like a falling star.

"You know," I started, "being here with you, it's kinda..." Victoria grabbed me, and kissed me, her arms strong, the smell of lilacs all over me, her hard nipples pressing against my chest. I responded zombie-like, taken aback by the passion in her. The embrace lasted for a long time. I ran my fingers over her shoulders, hot to the touch, ending up inside the back of her shorts, feeling the band of her panties there, silky, not the cottony athletic issue I would have imagined. If I'd imagined, but I hadn't. Now here she was, her sunburned skin tingling hot under my hands. After a moment, I pushed my tongue against her lips, into her mouth; it opened wide.

A loud belch, a big raw laugh. Ziggy. I looked up, saw the guys stumbling down the stairs, lit by the cottage veranda lights, beers in hands.

"Duck!" I whispered. We slid down on the big back seat, as they made their way past the car down to the river. I felt her heart beating against my chest, her breathing a little ragged.

"You really going to swim, Stan?" Ron asked.

"It'll be refreshing, fer fuck's sake."

"River rash, leeches, yeah, that's refreshing."

"River rash my ass, you fuckin' jamtart."

"Where's that Dick prick anyway? He's missing all the fun." They laughed as they walked past the car and disappeared into the darkness.

We were alone again, in silence. "Thought you hated me?" I said.

Victoria sat up. "Yeah?" She looked out the window.

Could it be that she liked me, wanted me? All that hostility, her glaring and her sarcasm: was it some kind of flirting? With me? Was I really lovable?

"You're beautiful," I whispered in her ear, biting it gently, surprised by my words as I said them and yet realizing, out of the moment, that they were perfectly serious then and there. She looked at me, full in the face, and kissed me again. I smelled Noxzema on her skin.

For a while we got lost in each other, kissing and touching, eyes closed. But then:

"Come *on*. Jesus, these cock-sucking bugs—I'm closin' the door, hurry up, *hurry*, keep 'em out!" It was Ron, followed by the guys. One by one they clumped drunkenly past the car, up the steps, into the cottage. Victoria and I breathed into each other wordlessly. The screen door slapped shut.

She sat up, smoothed back her hair, pulled down her top. "Well. I better go. My folks will wonder."

"What—"

"Call me, in town." She slid out of the car into the darkness. I leaned over the front driver's seat and yanked the headlight switch: her pink top was a beacon moving down the road. She turned, waved.

I hit the light off, lit another smoke, sat staring at the moon until the cigarette burnt my fingers. Then I went in. But I didn't say anything to the guys about what happened. I had this crazy feeling that they wouldn't believe it, anyway, think I was putting them on—and I wouldn't blame them; it seemed unbelievable to me too. Besides, it was private. I was numb with excitement, exhilarated yet bewildered, like some law of nature had been repealed. For the rest of the night I played poker badly, losing all my money without much concern.

At one point, after a particularly stupid bet by me, Ron said: "On your walk, did aliens eat your brain, by any chance?"

"Uh—guess I'm just tired; I'm turning in." The guys stared at me hard as I stumbled off to bed. But I could not sleep. Had Victoria been hot for me all this time and I was just too dumb to notice? Was she betraying her best friend? Did it matter? Was this really bizarro, or just something "adult," normal? Were all women so unpredictable? Who did

I want, anyway? The Polish Princess or the Lady in Waiting? It went round and round until dawn.

Back in town, I started doubting what had happened with Victoria that night. Maybe I had been a little drunk, drunk enough to imagine more than had happened, reading too much into our time together. Maybe it was all a joke, her getting back at me—then she'd tell Wanda for revenge. Or, maybe, *she* would call *me?*

After three days of uncertainty and feverish speculation, I gave up, and picked up the phone: "Victoria there?"

"Who is it?" Her mom answered, with a distinct English accent.

"A friend, from school."

"She'll be gone for about another week, maybe longer. Her grandmother is ill…in Toronto. Victoria's taking care of her until she's recovered, if—"

"Oh. Can I leave a message? It's Richard."

"Certainly."

But I did not hear from Victoria as the summer dragged into its final weeks of sweat-soaked bus-swabbing. Nor did the Polish Princess get in touch, as she said she would when back from Detroit. I thought of calling, imagined her parents' icy voices on the phone, and didn't; it felt over. As for the guys, it was sort of like that, too; we never went back to the cottage for another card-playing weekend, and started instead going our separate ways. Stan and his steady set a date for the wedding. It was like my lie, or rather silence, about what had happened on my walk had registered somehow, changed our dynamic.

I had put off telling my parents about my expulsion from St. Paul's—their limited English gave me an enjoyable control over that sort of information, and so far the time just hadn't felt right. Now September was here, school was back in session and I wasn't registered anywhere. I pretended that St. Paul's had just now dropped me, withdrawing my scholarship for reasons unknown; the narrative fit into my mother's world view of rich powerful people victimizing innocent Poles like us, and she bought it, getting loud and red-faced at the injustice. My dad puffed on a smoke, turned away to look out the window as I pitched my story, how it was too late to get my traumatized rejected Polish self into grade eleven now, as public schools went back weeks earlier than private, how my summer gig at Grey Goose was over and there were hundreds of great-paying jobs in Calgary and Toronto just waiting for someone industrious like me. (This last part was semi-true—except that I felt way too restless to sign up for anything, school or any real kind of work.)

With almost a thousand dollars in my savings account for the first time, and my parents' half-hearted agreement, I traveled, not anywhere fascinating like overseas, but to places that were new and exotic to me: grey Toronto, then wet balmy Vancouver, where roses grew in back alleys, and finally Calgary, crashing with people I hardly knew, getting a few days' work here and there, hanging out in the bar car of the CP Transcontinental, or bouncing around in the back of a Greyhound, staring at scenery, hitting Winnipeg every few months for a solid dose of pyrogies with my family, drifting.

Just moving seemed crucial, being ceaselessly on the go, as if I were looking for something, some kind of grail. As I traveled, my back-seat minutes with Victoria went with me. I'd look out a Greyhound window after dark, seeing my ordinary face reflected back in flashes against the black outer world, and relive our time together, think about the mystery of her sudden sweetness, her laughter, her passion directed to me like an undeserved gift that summer night.

In a sense, of course, my night with Victoria was nothing—a couple of teens in a car necking. What could be less important? And I never followed up on my call to her, even when I was back in Winnipeg for a few days of solid eating, afraid maybe to risk my radiant memory of that night. As it turned out, I never saw her again. Yet, in another way it *was* important; with her touch, her sudden kiss, my world had shifted, become full of freedom, forgiveness and possibility instead of constricting patterns—you just had to be ready, open, to recognize opportunity when it came. Was that the meaning, the truth inside my wanderlust?

The haloed lights of some little town flew by the bus window, now steamed-over and half-obscured by my breath; I stared at them, watched them disappear—maybe somewhere out there was a place in which I could be my weird, goofy, flawed self and, just for that, be loved.

Movies on the Moon

We were driving through St. James down Portage towards the western end of town, in my dad's aging 1964 Pontiac Custom Sport. It was a windy night in January, minus 25°F, snow swirling in the headlights, spiraling down and around in that way that can make you a little dizzy, tires crunching on the hard-pack beneath them, car heater buzzing warm on stiff booted toes—then suddenly pink seashells on a sunny Caribbean beach and a bikinied Ursula Andress, 30 feet tall, almost nude but stately, like a regal princess from a primitive tribe, filling the opaque sky, her acres of golden flesh wiping out Winnipeg.

The first feature of a third-run James Bond double-bill had already started. But that was OK. We hadn't even checked the paper to see what was playing. It didn't matter; this was the only show in town. An hour ago I'd been sitting at home with Mom and Dad, fake-studying for my university course, breathing in the dry furnaced air, monitoring a faint thudding in my head. Then the phone rang, beginning our Tuesday night ritual.

"So what are you doing?"

"Nothing."

"You?"

"Nothin'."

"Want to go?"

"Sure."

I picked up Ron. Stan and Bogdan couldn't make it this particular night, so it was just the two of us. We swung into a beer parlour on Ellice, where they weren't such sticklers about age as at the government liquor stores, picked up a twelve-pack of Molson Canadian plus some Matinées, and headed through the sparkling snow to the outdoor Odeon at the city's western edge.

In winter going to an outdoor movie wasn't for love, not like summer when I'd be there with a date and an agenda. Things were less romantic in January. Even if you could get a girl to go, the noisy heater, cold car seats, and multiple layers of clothing discouraged female passion. Being here tonight addressed other yearnings. Winter prairie nights are long and black, relentless from 5:00 p.m. to 9:00 a.m. Not much to do—you could maybe shoot some pool, get coffee in a diner, or go to a movie. That was the Peg, my hometown in timeless thrall to some evil force, the place where nothing happened. It was hopeless; the signs that welcomed travelers on the Perimeter Highway had held steady forever at "pop. 500,000"—I lived in a flat world where nothing, not even the population, grew. There were only three TV channels. That's why I went to the drive-in with buddies on those dead-end Tuesdays—to get out, escape one more night of trappedness.

As always, once parked, we tested several of the drive-in's in-car heaters, seeking the rare one that didn't roar like a tractor, and matched it to a full-functioning speaker. At first we positioned the heater in the middle of the front seats pointed upward, to warm noses and ears; later it would be aimed down to prevent frostbitten toes. It was cold either way. A side window had to be kept ajar for the speaker wire plus heater cord with its clunking anti-theft chain, and to vent smoke from our non-stop cigarettes. At eye level the opening let in a stab of Arctic wind, which, along with the heater never quite withstanding the sub-zero temperature, meant we had to run the car every fifteen minutes to keep the interior bearable. These periodic blasts of heat also de-fogged a rounded centre portion of the windshield.

The week before it had been *Barbarella*, the week before that *The Wild Bunch*. As I sat, icy beer chilling my hands and innards, straining to catch the cool Bond dialogue above the crackle and hum of heater and car noise, scenes from those films drifted through my mind: Barbarella innocently breaking the "orgasmetron," then fleeing the killer dolls with their snapping white-toothed jaws; the final suicidal slo-mo shootout in which Peckinpah's bunch slaughters hundreds, blood spurting everywhere. Something, maybe the cold, made these images stand out sharp as colour snaps on a page, not like the fuzzed, fleeting memories retained from indoor viewing. Or was it just because we always parked way up front, in the third or fourth row, eager for the full, overwhelming effect of the huge open-air screen? It towered into the sky, above the windshield top, making my neck hurt after only a few minutes into the film but worth the ache.

We seemed alone, as if the show was being put on specially for us; there were only six cars in the lot behind ours, huddled near the concession as if for mutual warmth. The colossal screen blotted out the city, replaced it with enormous floating faces and bodies glowing bright as novas in the vacuum of frozen dark.

For the first hour it kept snowing, fat white feathers that disappeared once they drifted into the glowing light of the projected film. The lazy, wind-buffeted flakes framed the moving images on all sides, like TV screen "snow" except on the outside of the TV. When it stopped falling, stars started to wink around the screen, once our eyes adjusted to the dark beyond the glare of the giant rectangle of reflected light that was being bounced back at us.

The Molson made me weightless and woozy. Near the end of *Dr. No*, I noticed a milli-second lag between what I thought and said, like in those TV clips of astronauts playing on the Moon while talking to Earth. The muzzed soundtrack added to a growing sense of jolly disorientation. My doubled socks, Stanfield's long johns, flannel shirt, and wool sweater under a heavy fur-lined parka—plus mitts—felt like a bulky spacesuit. At intermission we went to use the john and get some food, our movements slowed and flattened into a cartoon of normal human body gestures by the padded clothes and effects of beer. I lurched like Neil Armstrong across a monochromatic moonscape, bounced off the mounds and ridges of icy snow formed by cars parking. We laughed out loud.

There was no lineup at the concession stand. Unlike in summer, it was empty, a cave of dead white neon. Two shivering girls huddled behind the counter, serving up pre-cooked fast food, dark heavy sweaters under their white uniform tops making them look fat. The fare was grim. When I pulled a lukewarm steamed hot dog out of its slippery foil pouch for doctoring, it emerged a congealed mass of wienie and bun, too stuck together for decent condiment spreading. Long and lank, it flopped over in my hand in a big sad C. Likewise my pale wan fries were in a clammy lump that made proper ketchup application impossible. Ron's bun came half off, stuck to its wrapper; he shrugged, slapped a dollop of bright yellow mustard on the exposed meat and re-sealed the cheeseburger.

Nothing worked quite right in winter at the drive-in. Before getting the food, I'd tried to flush a toilet—nothing happened. Maybe the pipes were frozen. Back in the car, as we wolfed down our soggy meal before it chilled completely, the speaker abruptly went wonky, emitting an endless unbearable high-pitched whine. Unlike in July, when you could easily tune into the soundtrack from other speakers because of wide-open windows, now there was no carry-over from other cars; sounds got lost in the frigid air.

But it didn't really matter. We switched the speaker off, sat staring in silence. The show went on: blazing images, brilliant colours, car chases and fights, 007 outsmarting SPECTRE in style. I realized, though, that I was getting a little tired of the long drawn-out underwater sequences that dominate *Thunderball*.

The car smelled of mustard. I popped another beer, looked at Ron sprawled beside me: "Kinda weird, eh, sitting here, freezing our butts off in the dark?" I said.

He rolled down his window, took a final drag on his Matinée and flicked it out. The pinpoint of burning light shot skyward toward the exit way, then arced down, disappearing into the snow. "Nah," he said thoughtfully. "It's cool. Like being in outer space."

Yeah... And I was the *Canadian* astronaut, bounding out to the concession, braving a potentially killing atmosphere, breath clouding the indifferent stars. This was the True North, defying the elements to sit huddled in a car before the monolithic screen, to suffer, to bring food and drink and commune that night with gods. Who knew what tomorrow would bring? It was the late sixties, and every day the news seemed full of death. Hendrix, Joplin, the FLQ, Vietnam. What about me? The immortal moving images on the screen went on, unscathed by time, cold, circumstance, through endless Night. I had to be there, at the improbable winter drive-in, exposed in frozen darkness, teetering on the edge of the Precambrian Shield that centred the continent, absurd yet exhilarated, watching a movie on the moon, huddled in front of the monolithic screen, seeing the magic play of giant images brilliant against the sky, sparks of creativity—like flashes of living thought—jumping galvanically in the black and soulless void.

MIDNIGHT MOM

There was no real curfew for me when I was a teenager; my mother's rule was simple: I could stay out as late as I wanted Saturday night, as long as I was ready for mass at 8:00 the next morning.

When I'd get home I'd find her shut in the living room, lying on the chesterfield under a blanket, watching TV with the sound low to avoid disturbing my father and brother, though that wasn't really necessary as both were solid sleepers. The room was lit only by the ghostly glow from the black and white screen, casting shadows over the furniture, walls, and the large ornately gilded frame of a Gainsborough print hanging on one of them, an image that dominated the room despite being wildly out of sync with the rest of the Polish folk-art decorations in the house.

I'd open the living room door quietly to catch the profile of her face in repose, watching intently what most often was a war movie. For a moment, in the still of the night, she would not know that I was there, looking at her. Then she'd turn and smile in secret recognition.

That's the picture, how I always remember her. Why? It's not her at her actual best. She was normally gregarious, a high-energy woman who liked most of all to entertain at home, to be surrounded by people who appreciated her "gifts," serving forth at table the traditional foods she loved to prepare for family and friends, even strangers. And she was generous. Often I'd walk in after school and find beggars at the front door. Other times it would be a Native Indian trying to get bus fare to go back to his reservation, the Fuller Brush guy, or the Mennonite farmer who delivered chickens and eggs. Whoever came would soon be hunkering down to a late lunch or early dinner with gusto. It didn't matter what time of the day; a hot meal was always just minutes away—being served up by my mom flushed with happiness, laughing, talking, enjoying the social context of "the visit." Then there were the frequent parties, dinners for old friends, new immigrants, distant family members. Once my handsome youngish uncle, when down on his luck, stayed for nine months without a question ever being asked. She was happy to have him.

But instead of as the beaming hostess she often was, I see her in the dark, alone, her image outlined by that weird faintly pulsing electronic light. She couldn't sleep because of the aches and pains in her legs, arms, abdomen—everywhere really, but mostly, I think, in her head. TV was one of her "little helpers," along with various painkillers she consumed hourly, to get her through until dawn, when she would rise on tired limbs once again and lose herself in the ceaseless daily physicality of cooking, cleaning, shopping, working, doing something, always moving. Her pain, psychic or not, was real and chronic, manifesting itself as various ailments needing treatment over the years, and she struggled always with controlling it. As long as I can remember she was on a steady diet of pills: 222s, 292s, Tylenol, sedatives, tranquilizers, Fioronal, Percodan, and many other medications. After a time we lost track of what she was taking and for what complaints. Once I came back from the coast for a visit to discover that she had undergone shock treatment and did not recognize me at the back door; no one had told me, or maybe they didn't know. Years later I discovered that she used to get morphine injections two, three times a week, right in the comfort and privacy of her home. The family physician, a countryman sympathetic to her immigrant history, would stop by on his way home at the end of the day and give her a shot. (When he died in the 1980s, it was a catastrophe, her only source of assured relief gone forever.)

So there she'd be at midnight every time I came home, watching TV. This was the sixties, early seventies, before colour, cable, and satellite. For a while, only one channel—the CBC—had a late show. My mother viewed whatever was on, weeknight or weekend: Bogart, Busby Berkeley, Hitchcock, cowboys, Charlie Chan. But the war flicks were her favourite—whether it was John Wayne single-handedly overrunning the Philippines, or Jack Hawkins stoically captaining a ship in the North Atlantic. It didn't matter. Or did it? Was there something about those movies—not the stories they told so much as the general and specific culture of war they bodied forth—that resonated in her soul? Maybe their imagery gave shape to a mysterious cyclic memory process about her own wartime experiences on which her mind was stuck, like a needle on a flawed vinyl LP—narratives expressed repeatedly in her day-to-day conversations with family, friends, and even to complete strangers on the street, or to the passersby she invited in and fed. There was something there, something odd. Whenever she met someone new, as I learned with ever-increasing embarrassment during my self-conscious teen years, within two minutes she'd be talking in exalted, excruciatingly revelatory terms about the war, her voice moving up and down the octave as she expanded on her own gory details, stuff I'd heard a thousand times, and how it had changed her life. She needed to speak the horrible truth, to tell *her* story to the world, like some fixated Ancient Mariner babbling in broken English. And there was no stopping her.

One war movie my mother really liked was *Ice Cold in Alex* (1958), with John Mills as the semi-alcoholic Captain Anson trying to get a motley band made up of two nurses (one played by Sylvia Syms), a Sergeant Major (Harry Andrews), and a charming hitchhiker they pick up who turns out to be a German spy (Anthony Quayle), safely through a German offensive, across the Sahara to Alexandria. It's set in a monochromatic, hellishly empty desert, the perfect backdrop for the Mills character to get shakier and edgier in close-ups the more setbacks the group endures. He fantasizes about an ice-cold beer in his favourite Alexandrian watering hole; the memory of a tall glass of Pilsner on the bar, with beads of condensation glistening down its sides, is his lodestar.

At the time I didn't understand what my mother liked so much about this film, but now I think she probably identified with the lead character: the struggle to keep going under the difficult circumstances of war may have been much like her own.

When I'd come home on those movie nights, the house felt solid, safe, and welcoming, with good smells from my mother's day-long cooking. Something was always on the stove, simmering. In the kitchen a small night light shone reassuringly on the top, next to a pot of chicken soup or *bigos* cooling down for transfer to the fridge. I'd join her in the living room, come in to her to say hello, maybe recount my evening adventures, depending on how law abiding they had been. Then I'd tune into the movie, keeping company, for unlike my father and brother, I was not a good sleeper, and the dread of school in the morning added to my developing insomnia (another thing we had in common).

It was oddly comforting to enter my mother's midnight world. The room was warm and close in the dark, especially after the deep white freeze of Winnipeg winter. And there was a well-established pattern to our late-night rendezvous. Usually, unless the pain was especially bad, she became more mellow toward the end of the day, drugged perhaps into a more relaxed state of being. Supper at home was always early, especially in winter, around 5:00, so by midnight we were both a little peckish. I'd make tea for her, a snack for both of us, a beer for me and, later on, a cognac for her. It had to be pricey Courvoisier V.S.O.P.; this was another of her "medicines," and no other brandy could be substituted. In all things she was paradoxical, at once extravagant and thrifty, putting out lots of cash for things like fine brandy, alligator handbags, and fur coats (she had six, probably worth half what our fairly plain house was valued at), but frugal to the point of self-punishment when it came to things like taking a bus, walking miles instead in the icy Winnipeg wind (wrapped in one of her furs) to save a few cents. Or scrimping to send parcels to her Polish relations, then at Christmas buying the most beautiful and expensive ornaments available to hang on our scrappy three-dollar tree.

Late at night we'd sit in the companionable darkness, eating, drinking, watching, while the rest of the family and most of the city slept. Beyond the TV set in front of the picture window, through the partly open curtains, I saw the lights of our neighbours' houses blink out one by one, and the traffic thin to the occasional car and taxi. Our movie fix was partly based on a long history of film-going by just the two of us. My father never did that sort of thing, nor my brother (he was too young at that time). My mother and I used to march summer and winter, a couple of miles each way, in order to cut down on the expense, out to the theatre on Selkirk Avenue. She would bring along a smelly smoked meat sandwich, buried deep in her purse, for us to share instead of putting out money for popcorn.

When we finally got a TV, apparently there was no longer any need for my mother to go *out* to see a film. There were plenty of war movies on late at night. But things were different at home; it wasn't much of a video experience anymore. Inevitably, the narrative spell was broken a few minutes after the opening credits, as my mother started to talk over it, every movie, obsessively about the war, her worst and best of times, her touchstone of drama and history. Somehow the on-screen images summoned up the minutiae of the great central adventure and mystery of her life—how she had been swept up into the war by occupying forces, never again to see her family or home in rural Poland.

I used to think my mother watched these war movies avidly because she needed documentation, some verifiable vindication of her chaotic past, a reference point. She needed the record to show clearly what had happened in the war as far as she understood it through her own personal history. Often, she would "argue" with the movies we were watching, insisting that the story was wrong, that Poles were not justly or correctly represented in the story, and so on. With the sophisticated wisdom of my late teens and early twenties, I tried to help her with the distinction between fact and fiction, to explain that movies are not necessarily "true" in that way, but to no avail; she refused to be informed by me, demanded irrefutability and was outraged by its continued absence.

That is what I thought then. But one particular night, everything shifted. The CBC had started to put what they advertised as "film festivals" in the late night slot, on innocuous Tuesdays, I think. Once it was all Bogart. Then French classics, like Jean Renoir's features. And then came post-war Polish films, which had a high profile in those days, like Wajda's symbolic trilogy that ends with *Ashes and Diamonds* (1958). These had not been previously available to us in Winnipeg; I had only recently heard of them. So I was excited. At last, I thought, my mother would be satisfied once and for all, seeing her tumultuous history confirmed in her own language and from her unique nationalist perspective in movies made by her people, who had gone through a similarly painful upheaval and survival process.

I anticipated the interesting conversations we'd have after these Tuesday night viewings; maybe I'd learn more about my family's history and get a better understanding of my mother's life-changing wartime experience—that could only be good. And perhaps it would be cathartic for her, in some way, I hoped.

On the first night, I ordered a pizza for delivery, an unusual occurrence at our home. After decades of decrying the wastefulness of those who ate out, my mother had begun to crave certain North American convenience foods. It was a treat. I put out the usual brandy and beer; the pizza arrived, and the show started.

My mother listened to the Polish words spoken while white subtitles flickered like snakes across the bottom of the screen. Then after a minute or two she started talking over the soundtrack as usual, the usual stuff: telling the same old horror stories, making the familiar complaints, negating the film narrative with her own story that I had heard so many times before.

At first I tried to redirect her to what was on the screen, urging the "genuine" Polishness of it on her. Soon enough, though, I realized she didn't care. It might as well have been another John Wayne battle epic. Or whatever. It was all the same to her. For her the range of war movies blended into one homogeneous apocalyptic story, not history per se but a mythic realm of conflict, permanent in the world at large and in her mind in particular. And certain things came together then in my mind that I had never understood about her. For instance, I remembered her romantic enthusiasm about the well-turned-out German armies of 1940—when they invaded Poland—as opposed to the slovenly Russian armed forces. She had spoken in an approving, accepting way, as if it were merely normal that nations went to war and some were less appropriately fitted for it than others; as if it were a matter of etiquette and fashion.

Or maybe there was a war movie running in her head *all* the time, a personal one just about her, not the larger world. And of course no movie could ever match that inner reality. That's when I saw it, that a gulf existed between us, her and me, and her and the rest of the family, never to be bridged. Her ongoing movie *was* her, the way she defined herself: in an endless loop of inhabited experience, relived daily, a psychic framework more real than actuality. Release from its grip was impossible. There was nothing she *wanted* to understand about the world, her personal "great war," her role in it, or even her own demons; there was no need to, and all the other war movies were mere wallpaper.

Sometimes now, when I can't sleep, I switch on the TV late at night, go to the History Channel to find a documentary (preferably with black and white footage) about the war. Any war will do. Usually I leave the sound off, not because I'm afraid to wake anyone, but because I want to lose myself in images, in their historical permanence. I watch guns shooting, bombs falling, explosions, marching armies, soldiers mugging at the camera, ships sailing away, tanks rolling, and I sense my mother caught somewhere in the permanent celluloid, among the endless frames of death and destruction, forever at war with herself.

BACK TO BASICS?

Schools often look like prisons, I thought, driving on—too bad about that. It was the wrong thought for that particular morning, but you know how it is with job interviews. You start out more or less sane in the morning, then begin to question everything about your life, trying to figure out what you really want when/if you grow up, what went wrong along the way, where do you go from here, and so on. Interviews cast a spotlight you mostly want to avoid. As you look at the "paper you" black-inked onto your latest application package, it's hard not to interview yourself: what is the meaning of my life? Why did I buy this tie? Where am I headed? Should I stop? But that day I kept going, retracing my turns and twice passing a sign that told me I had entered the Raspberry Capital of Canada. Eventually I found my way to the Abbotsford

Campus of FVC for my interview. Oddly, the buildings did not look like a public lavatory, the way most institutions of medium-high learning do, perhaps for economic reasons, perhaps a specific academic aesthetic. Rather, encouragingly, this college looked like a kids' play castle, soft fairytale pink with pointy turrets and a clock tower that, in a playful manner, chose to tell different times on each of its four faces.

Inside the air-conditioned faculty and staff lounge, the department head puffed on a cigarette, blew smoke in the air, looked out the window at snow-capped Mount Baker, and said in her soft, slightly faltering voice: "OK...I guess. You start...on the fifteenth, or after. Depending, of course..."

Just me and her, chatting for less than half an hour. No committee. No test. No tension. It all seemed implausible, ambiguous, so I pressed for something, not sure what: reassurance, information, punishment? Some kind of reality check: "The students, ah...my students, they're from different program areas?"

"Yes, all kinds." She smiled enigmatically, then looked vaguer still, the White Queen from *Alice in Wonderland*. "You'll find things...different around here."

"Yeah?"

"Farming and jail—those are the main industries in the Valley." She laughed gently.

Ten days into term she called again, offering me another class, if I was—she paused as if seeking the perfect, hard-to-find word—"interested." I was, as was the collection agency that had now assumed ownership of my student loan account. And now I had a further chance, to parachute into a section on the eastern campus, taking over for a department member who had suddenly become ill, to establish myself further in this teaching career.

"They're aggies," the Head's voice continued softly through the phone, almost whispering in my ear—and then, after registering my perplexed silence: "In the agricultural program."

And that's how I became a peripatetic instructor, always on the go, relentlessly driving, one eye on the clock and the other on the speed. Listening to CBC Radio chat, the 10:00 a.m. tones, feeding tapes into the maw of the car's deck—John Klemmer, The Pretenders. Suspended in time, safe but adrift driving through the Valley, and then, at the end of the day, zooming back home to the city.

I mostly found the commute intriguing, not frustrating, the way things slowed down as I went into the Valley to work, from one extreme to the other. In a relatively short drive there were big differences in landscape, climate, and temperament, not to mention temperature. It was always hotter or colder in the Valley—because it was clearer there, less cloudy—differences great enough that sometimes I'd take a change of clothes, especially when facing a long day with an evening class. In the late summer/early fall I'd travel from gentle coastal warmth to Valley heat and then back to ocean breeze cool. Then, as winter approached I'd go from rain at home to snow sometimes in Abbotsford and more in Chilliwack, to ice and slush and hail-slick roads. Something in me liked these contrasts, the quick drama, the sense of a real, if small, journey undertaken—all so different from what I'd known for most of my life in Winnipeg and its two seasons, the six months of solid, implacable freeze followed by blazing heat.

Term buzzed along. Classes were going fine, even the Native students with whom I felt least surefooted were quietly responsive—my confidence was growing daily, and the aggie section I had now signed up to sub for would be no problem.

A meeting with the ailing instructor was scheduled beforehand, to get me up to speed. "Cancer," she said, in a matter-of-fact Valley sort of way. "I'll be in treatment the next four months—won't be back this term."

Her students were offspring of European immigrants for the most part, she told me, Dutch, German, Slav, etc., who had settled in the Valley; their parents had worked the land and prospered. Kind of like my folks back in the Peg, I said, except for the prospering part. She expressed some concern about having to stop teaching almost mid-term, but I assured her that we—her students and I—would get along just fine, bonded by our shared "immigrant persuasion." She looked out the window, wished me good luck.

When I went home that night my answering machine was flashing—a long-distance call from my mother. Her odd blend of Polish and Ukrainian sounded even odder after the sundry buzzes, bleeps and musical cues of the Japanese-designed, Mexican-built, North American-style respond-o-matic. She never seemed to accept the notion that what she heard was just a recorded message, not me talking to her live, so as always I heard her beseeching me, repeating my name as if I were in fact standing there, monitoring the call. Which, to be fair, I had been, at times. But now I phoned back quickly, stimulated by the notion of teaching a class of younger versions of myself, youths who could benefit not only from my recently acquired M.A. and even more recent info on business letters and memo formats, but also from our shared experience of being both outsiders and insiders in Canada. My talk with Mom was brief but satisfying, as she was proposing to send out a care package including a smoked turkey—delicious, and unattainable in Vancouver in those days—and some of my favourite rhubarb jam cookies, the ones that look like miniature croissants sprinkled with cinnamon sugar. She was happy to hear that I had more work and promised extra kielbasa in the package. Having arranged the pickup details, I hung up, wolfed down some leftover stir fry and rice straight from the fridge, and fell asleep to dream of classrooms where I was both teacher and student and the sun shone like honey through the windows…

Then I met the class. The aggies… True enough, some of them looked vaguely like me in that German, Ukrainian, Polish, Russian sort of way, florid, broad-faced, many of them fair haired. But twenty minutes into the first class it was clear: no fellow feeling there. I tried, but this particular group on the eastward campus seemed against me from the start. At first I told myself it was temporary, a natural reaction to losing their familiar teacher, the shock of her sudden illness, a drastic shift of routine and expectation, upheaval six weeks into their course. All a challenge to my maturity—a surmountable challenge, of course.

But no. The bad feeling didn't pass. The weather cooled, the temperature in class grew frostier still, and it all felt personal. Far from any sense of fellow immigrant feeling, my being an outsider here meant being not a Pole or a Manitoban but a Vancouverite, and that was a very bad thing. Too late I realized that telling them where I lived, how I wasn't familiar with the Valley and needed to get to know it, was my first big mistake; a wave of disdain was directed at me at once. My next strategy, trying to reach out to them on a peer basis, as some sort of Slav or European type, was equally sneered at, equally doomed; my "sharing" questions about communication style differences in ethnic groups, and about changing family names to fit in or not, got nothing but stony silence.

Every class with them was tense, a minor ordeal. Twice a week I felt their resentment and it hurt. They were a tight-knit cohort group, socializing on the weekends, sharing rides to college, and so on; now a shared dislike of me became their ultimate bonding experience. I wasn't much of a lecturer (still am not), and with no rapport, there was no dialogue in our classroom, no laughs, no learning through play. I started to not like them very much, and began wondering about the whole enterprise of teaching students who despise their teacher. As a student, I had been for the most part inspired by my instructors (despite a few notable exceptions), to the point of wanting to follow in their footsteps. What, then, was wrong with me? The other classes I was teaching were great, this one horrible. Yet this was the one that dominated my consciousness, and of course I couldn't get out of it, especially after all the enthusiasm I had initially voiced—how could I, without declaring myself the complete failure that, with them, I was? And yet, was it worth anything, other than a paycheque at the end of the month? Was I really a teacher at all, or just a big mistake?

There was a ray of sunshine. One highly articulate girl, the only bright spark of the bunch, made it worth coming to class, worth marking the papers. Though quiet and "little-brown-hen" in style, she, Margery, was a simply beautiful writer, stylish, witty, a pleasure to read. Naturally I praised her writing, her ideas, her impressive skills with argument and structure; but marks like 9 out of 10, leaving some margin for perfection, upset her. She needed explanations, lots of explanations of every dot of coloured ink on her pages. We spent hours poring over individual assignments in the office, as if they were complex treasure maps, or translations from a long-dead tongue, instead of straightforward, brief writing assignments that had already received an A or A+. At the end of each accounting session she would be, not stimulated like a keen writing student who had learned something about her work, but sad, vaguely cross, exhausted. Even stranger, when I once gave her a mark of 6 out of 5 to recognize how she'd gone above and beyond expectation, she wasn't happy with that either. To my shock I found her looking at me sorrowfully when she got her paper back, as if I'd transgressed some mystical marking precept and made a fool of her.

Meanwhile the rest of that class deteriorated further in terms of our teacher-student dynamic. Now, after four weeks together, I felt these students didn't want to learn *anything*, at least not from me, and were simply hunkered down to get passed on through. I tried to be open, flexible, accommodating, all that good stuff. Nothing worked. Even small things became big problems. For instance, my "real world" examples were drawn not from the Valley, naturally enough, but from elsewhere. I'd used them in other communications classes with fair success; here the students hated them. One day, I mentioned what I felt was a fascinating fact: in terms of population, *L.A.* was actually Canada's fifth largest city.

For a moment the aggies looked blank, then one of the guys, blond and beefy in a blue lumberjack shirt, snapped, "So what?"

Right. By now I was dreading every drive eastward beyond Abbotsford. Aggie students were waiting there, waiting to disbelieve whatever I had to say, waiting to argue every word, every point, as if we were in a court of law, as if I were their enemy, forcing them to do something awful against their will. The class space, in one of the temporary portable rooms, was itself unnerving. Every step I took at the blackboard produced loud embarrassing creaking noises like something from the Addams Family, ironic sound effects for the falsity of our situation.

The only thing that made the drive to Chilliwack tolerable was that bright girl, the good writer—sure, she was demanding, but she was also what kept me going through each class. Then, one day, she wasn't there, and never came again. Given our odd sessions over every returned paper, I should have expected this, but I didn't and was crushed, all the more so because she said nothing to me, just stopped showing up. Despite the general hostility of the group, as the days went by I couldn't stand not knowing, and queried one of the less daunting students who told me—to my astonishment—that Margery had dropped my course because she was afraid "she wasn't going to get an A." The only student in the group who would have! Another irony, but once again not in that enjoyable Eng Lit way.

One cold shadowy winter afternoon near the end of term, when I was happily thinking that my time with the aggies would soon be over, someone knocked softly on my office door.

"It's not locked," I said, looking up from the papers I was grading.

And Margery slid in. She sat on the extreme edge of the designated visitor chair and apologized for having dropped out without letting me know. Pressures at home, she said, had made been making life difficult—I nodded, pleased to hear it wasn't really, shallowly, about grades, and she settled back more comfortably.

As the room darkened we kept talking for a long time, maybe an hour, about her family situation, her perfectionism; she was articulate as always. Mostly I listened...to Margery's extended, almost clinical analysis of her "issues," how they were all wrapped up in her mother's love—love not for her, the daughter, but for the younger brother who could do no wrong, in her mom's eyes at least. I was impressed anew by Margery's vocabulary ("empowerment," "self-loathing," "narcissism" all in the same sentence) and by her evident self-awareness.

Then she got to the reason for this visit, her request: could she make a speech to the class, as part of the final presentations which concluded the term? After all, they—the class—had been together for a couple of years and were quite close, actually, and she needed to share something important with them.

"What?" I asked.

She paused for a moment, looked away, then answered that she was anorexic and wanted to warn her classmates of the telltale signs of this illness, so they might be able to help someone close to them because, after all, the problem was epidemic. It would be a public-spirited gesture, she suggested, as well as a species of private reconciliation.

Despite her persuasive pitch, it seemed odd, with her having dropped out of the course and all; and I had a full slate of presentations for the final class. On the other hand, wasn't there something positive about her desire to do this, to seek some completion? No doubt the class had been further thrown off by her unexpected departure on top of my parachuting in; maybe her gesture could be redemptive for all, a kind of bonding experience that might finally draw me in as well—they'd see that I was an OK guy, open to their unique needs, in my way one of them. They might even begin to like instead of loathe me before our time together came to its much-desired end—and, though I hated to admit it to myself and it made no sense at all, more and more I found myself desperate for some tiny sign of friendliness, or at least tolerance, from this group.

Most of all, of course, it would help this talented girl with the health problem that she was bravely trying to confront. I looked at her covertly, hoping she was on the road to recovery from her terrible illness; to me she appeared all right, maybe a little pale and bundled up in a brownish Cowichan sweater...but in the dim light it was hard to really tell.

Then I said, "Well, if there's time left at the end, OK," and we agreed that she would attend the last class in any case, waiting to see how long things went.

When the last class with the aggies came, Margery sat patiently in the back row. There was plenty of time, as it turned out, since most of the students made rudely perfunctory presentations, the kind where all the research is from *Webster's Dictionary*. The audience chatted throughout the lacklustre speeches, then cheered and applauded, awarding each and every one an "A" on their group assessments. When the last guy finished his three-minute report on why sports are good (because they are, was his basic argument), I introduced Margery. She took the podium, standing next to it, not behind, and began a mesmerizing, perfectly structured discourse on anorexia in general and her specific history in particular.

Within a few seconds the chattering, unruly class fell dead silent. Margery's former classmates squirmed and looked down, uncomfortable at being forced suddenly to confront disagreeable reality. With quiet confidence she called for questions, comments, and it was quickly clear that, like me, they'd had no idea of her ongoing health problems. Now Margery described where she'd been during those weeks away, how she'd been hospitalized repeatedly for anorexia and bulimia, endured the violation of forced feedings, almost died, and so on. They were shocked, gobsmacked by each new disclosure, and I could understand their reaction, especially since Margery did not look dramatically emaciated, maybe just a bit on the delicate side.

Margery talked calmly about her illness—intubations, vomitus, enemas, IV site infections, hiatal hernias—as her classmates cringed. After ten minutes or so she began to take her clothes off as she spoke: it was a trick, she explained in show-and-tell style, that anorexics used to disguise their true body appearance. She took off a khaki cardigan, then a brown sweater; a pair of beige chinos fell, leaving a brown pair underneath. As she disencumbered herself of more bulky mud-coloured layers I heard soft groans from class members. Undisturbed, she continued to give statistics and drop garments; several of the male students were half-covering their eyes now, looking floorward, flushing a dull, nervous red as the presentation proceeded with an evocative description of the slack, pallid, grotesquely skeletal bodies that anorexics conceal beneath their clothes.

Disconcertingly, there was no straightforward match-up between words and vision. Instead, the more Margery took off the better she looked. The students' groans were from our shared anxiety, I thought, fear of confronting the starved, abused, secret body, the concentration camp skin-and-bones that Margery had so vividly described. But with every garment shed she seemed to be turning into the opposite, a tanned and healthy-looking young woman, thin but not apparently wasted, and no longer a little brown hen: garbed, it was now increasingly apparent, in multiple underlayers of brightly coloured lingerie.

She said something about lesions, about tissue damage. Some gruesome unveiling must lie ahead—but when? Why wasn't it already evident to us? The contradiction between what we were hearing and what we were seeing made me feel dazed, as if something had gone wrong with my mind. Was it, as Margery's report indicated, that we were all so programmed by the media, by society, by misogyny, that we couldn't recognize a fellow human being dying from malnutrition before our very eyes? Or was this something else: semiotic striptease, mysterious revenge, perverse display, celebration of the Sacred Feminine and powers thereof?

From the back corner of the room I had a clear view of both the class members and the presenter. I looked at these students who had tormented me all term long; they were fidgeting, unhappy, ill at ease, especially the boys. For them this was no *Animal House* fantasy trip, no teenage turn-on. The feeling, the smell in that portable classroom was fear.

I felt afraid too, and sorry, for Margery, for the students, for myself. I was allowing this to happen and when one or more of these hostile students talked about it, as of course they would, I would no doubt be fired, or simply never invited back. So I should stop it, stop her, right now, this second. And yet...at last something *real* was happening in this classroom where my efforts to teach, to reach, had all been scorned and obstructed. Fear is a part of authentic learning and they *were* learning today, experiencing something at least.

By now Margery was down to a silky raspberry-coloured camisole and matching tap pants. Of course she was more demurely clothed than most girls at Kits Beach, but then, we weren't on a beach. Margery said calmly, conversationally, that a distant mother was often a contributing factor. She made excellent eye contact with her audience, though they tried to slide away from it. She was *persuasive*, a watchword for this course, and radiant with something, though I couldn't tell exactly what.

Margery went on: "And the most important point about anorexics—" Suddenly I felt a weird stab of primitive glee. Serve them all right, I thought, for not liking me and rejecting what I had offered. That was *my* important point. I looked at the boys' tense slumped bodies, unwillingly there, imprisoned. And serve me right, too, to get myself fired for letting this happen, for being so passive, for not winning them over, for losing the job that had made me feel like this, be like this, desperate, loveless, useless—after all, basically it's an act of faith and love, teaching, a communion.

Communion. Margery's hands hovered at the waistband of her tap pants. I stood up. The floor creaked loudly, and I said: "Thank you so much for your thoughtful presentation, Margery. We've learned a lot, but are running out of time..." She looked at me, picked up a sweater, began to put it back on.

And then we all, our whole class, clapped like crazy.

None of the students ever spoke of that final presentation to me, or, as far as I could tell, to anyone else. And I remained at the college, saw some of the boys, from time to time, in the hallways. Our eyes would meet, not with friendship, but with a secret understanding like a scar, the residue of something shared. Or so I thought.

WORDS OF MY BECOMING

You forget: The squeak and hollow crunch of the snow, the sub-zero air numbing your face as you walk down the street at night. And the too-bright days—crisp sun-filled mornings and blinding afternoons. No shadows. Sharp outlines of everyday life, stark details, black and white. Like a Dürer etching, though not of double-nosed witches or apocalyptic horsemen. For those, you have to look beneath the surface...

Twenty years of living on the west coast has spoiled me for prairie life. My eyes are used to the shroud of Vancouver mist that softens the North Shore's peaks, and the fuzzed golden air of California winter on the beach at Del Mar. On the western edge of the continent, the light is different from season to season, and nothing is what it seems; the world shifts in and out of focus, through "the half colours of quarter-things."

That's how I like it—not like here, in my almost-hometown. Every prairie city vista is a framed picture, drawing you into an elemental reality: straight line of land at the bottom, empty sky at the top, cartoon buildings and dark figures trapped between in a one-dimensional Flintstone reality. It is strange that everything can be so flat. At the edge of the city, you can see a thousand miles in any direction. But why do I feel like I am falling, tumbling through space, through time?

February 4, 1990. I have come for one extravagant weekend, to surprise my parents at their fiftieth wedding anniversary celebration, the golden one. That's tomorrow night, a happy conspiracy on the part of their old friends, the dozen or so men and women they met in the war—in Siberia, on the trek south to Egypt in 1941 where the Poles were formed into an army under British auspices, and in the DP camps in England after Armistice.

After the end of hostilities, my parents spent several years in England, recovering. Then I was born, and they tried to emigrate wisely. Brazil, Australia, Canada—anywhere except back to the homeland which was then under Russian rule. Ironically, they and their friends landed here, in the middle of the Canadian prairies, in a shadowless land of Siberian dimensions.

Unlike some of their comrades, my parents have never returned home, never gone back to the peaceful part of Poland where they grew up that has changed flags, back and forth, over the centuries. That's why old friends are so important. After forty-five years, this group of displaced Poles still see each other regularly, because there is no way back and yet they must not forget—anything.

February 5, 1940. That's when my parents were married. Fifty years ago, at the start of the war—a doubled anniversary, sort of. On the eve of their honeymoon, the Germans and Russians came with a surprise Ribbentrop-Molotov gift package: free ride to Siberia, twenty-three days crammed in a boxcar, rumbling across unscenic northern plains. And they were lucky to get sent to a slave labour camp. At first they had been separated: my father rounded up by the Germans, my mother picked up by the Russians. But he managed to jump a fence, run away, and rejoin his bride, thereby probably escaping a darker fate.

This is not history, all these so-verifiable facts; it is life ongoing in the present tense for the survivors. Glasnost does not warm their hearts much; when they gather, these displaced Poles still argue about which of the Allied leaders murdered General Sikorski—was it Stalin or Churchill? Today the Kremlin is lifting the curtain and baring its troubled soul. But for some, like my mother, who tried several times to make a pilgrimage home before Gorbachev, such changes come too late. Five of her six brothers were killed by the war, including one in the Warsaw Uprising. Other relations have predictably been dying of old age and ill health ever since, my mother's own mother only a few years ago. Every year, in fact, there has been less and less to go back for.

My presence at the celebration tomorrow is expected, taken for granted. *Solidarnosc.* That's the way things are, and not just at anniversaries. In Polish, you never say "goodbye"; you always say *do widzenia*, which means "until we see each other again." And tomorrow night I will be met with hugs and kisses—and words. In a language that is beautiful yet melancholy, romantic and even melodramatic at times, full of dramatic cadences and emotional signifiers. A language of broken dreams. The history of Poland since the sixteenth century, when its empire began to unravel, is one of loss, longing, and partitions under cruel dominations—and its language reflects that anguished evolution. Polish is not like English, with its eclectic diversity and almost infinite play of possibility to soften meaning; there is nothing cool about its web. As always, I will be drawn in, and begin to remember. All that was lost—but may, someday, somehow, be redeemed.

What characterizes the Polish imagination, I tell myself coolly as I walk the flat streets, is precisely this romantic yearning for—what?—revelation. I have no trouble understanding millennialism, how, in particular, the great majority of the people of Poland can be both Catholic and communist, believing in heaven in the sky and on earth at once. Such apocalyptic thinking is only natural, considering an unnatural history.

For some reason, these thoughts fill my head with icons of ancient art as I trudge the streets of modern Winnipeg. I see Rembrandt's painting that has come to be known as The Polish Rider, for example, as an emblem of my homeland's strange psychic orientation. There it is: the horse, muscles strained in anatomically correct detail (owing something to Dürer, no doubt), foreleg raised, urged on to the right; the rider, body-line arched in the opposite direction, right arm casually at the hip, the other aristocratically reining his powerful steed, eyes to the left foreground, fixed on an unseen goal ahead, face resolute, though with the hint of a smile; a mysterious light from the left shadowing a desolate end-of-time background.

The painting conveys a profound sense of expectation. Rider and horse are poised at the brink of nothingness and the apex of transformation, about to charge into perilous action and change forever the course of history. All the opposed tensions balanced in this evocative canvas apprehend a sense of visionary adventure and existential resolution. Unlike Dürer's apocalyptic riders, there is no hurry; in this cataclysmic moment of being a calm sense of culmination prevails.

Years ago, when I was younger, someone told me I resembled Rembrandt's enigmatic Polish Rider. Back at home that night I dug out my art books and found a copy of the painting, out of curiosity. Gazing on the image, for the first time I felt, with a shock of recognition, truly Polish...

But right now, on the night before the big anniversary party, I resist such fatalistic notions. I am cool, English, myself, anonymous and alone, walking the streets of a frozen city under a black sky, seeing how things have remained much the same, in my almost-hometown. A four-square kind of permanence fixes the city solidly in place, pinning it to the flat earth, forcing me to remember with every noisy step.

I walk familiar streets, but I don't really know my way. Like a DP—"displaced person"—that's me. My first language is Polish, but I don't speak it where I live on the coast. I have never been to the country of my origins, never known the grandparents and other relations that lived there. As I grew up, here, my "family" was made up of my parents and their wartime comrades. They were my "aunts"and "uncles," their children a confusion of "cousins"; that's how I referred to and thought of all of them. For a long time, until I was about fifteen, I did not even understand the nature of extended family, and, when I did, it was with a sense of loss.

I am still confused about where I come from and where I belong. The past is like quicksand. This prairie town is where I grew up, but my memory does not compute the information very well. Bad sectors have skewed my personal history; parts of my childhood are damaged, perhaps irretrievable—and maybe the truth is that I want it that way.

And then, the next night, I am at the party, standing at the head table, in the regulation basement rec room that has been set with long tables for a banquet. The eldest son come from far away to make funny speeches at the feast.

There is lots of food, too much, really. But in my family's circle, food is important communication. Dinner is a deliberate surfeit, an overabundance of traditional dishes, in order to celebrate—and to remember. Not a scrap is wasted, to show respect for the times when there was nothing to put on the table, or even a table. That's the way it is; every piece of bread sacred, to be broken in communion.

At 5:30, when we sat down, it was already night outside. At 10:00 we will eat again, a mostly cold supper of smoked meats and salads, and lots more *wodka*. That's what you do here, in Siberia, eat and drink often and heartily to keep out the cold and dark; I'd forgotten.

How it happens is always a surprise. When I get up to speak in my true language, at first stumbling over the rusty locutions, I can feel it start, the familiar pull. My body betrays me: fingers stabbing the air, arms waving dangerously, voice rising. It's as if my personality is transformed, taken over by a different yet familiar spirit. The words, now coming more easily, thanks to the *wodka*, pull me inevitably down and down.

My parents are genuinely surprised—by the party, my presence, and, I think, mostly by being alive after all the upheavals. My younger brother sits with us, on the other side of the head table, looking relaxed, a somewhat benign expression on his face. He does not get bothered the way I do by the inevitable reminiscing about the war that happens whenever these survivors get together, or at least that's how he appears.

"Don't worry about it," my brother says. "Let it go. You can't change them." He has a different perspective. Knowing the language more deeply, I have no perspective at all.

As I speak, I look out on my old "aunts" and "uncles"; we all know the truth. That one has just had his hips replaced with plastic sockets; this one is scheduled for spinal surgery next week. My father's left arm is increasingly atrophied, the legacy of a wartime bullet wound. And so time flies. They are all greyer, I see in the dimmed light of the room, as if fading from the colours of flesh and blood.

And, as I speak, seeing these familiar faces, I am overwhelmed by memories—

Out of the blue, I am ten or eleven years old again. At home on a Sunday, just before an "aunt" and "uncle" arrive for dinner. The room is full of light. I am lying on my bed, in my room, quietly reading *Mr. Midshipman Hornblower*, but I can hear everything happening in the house.

And my father is reclining on the couch in his usual Sunday afternoon resting mode, smoking, puffing clouds at the ceiling—no, not "couch"; they call it a "chesterfield" on the Prairies, in English, I mean. Then, at one o'clock, as he does every Sunday, my father turns on the radio for the weekly Polish news, broadcast from somewhere in the States, Chicago or Detroit.

Tuning noises. Static. Then thunderous chords of Chopin suddenly fill the house, that most romantic and dramatic polonaise that is the unofficial Polish national anthem. Martial, rousing, monumental music, not like Chopin's dances, meditative études or hypnotic nocturnes, nor like any anthem—this music is crashing, demanding attention, tearing at the heart. Then the announcer, speaking in words that make everything sound like the end of time.

I remember, but I keep talking, feeling my Polish words pull me still further down the pathways of memory. I tell my aging audience my memories of them—how this one bounced me on her knee, that one got me drunk on a beer when I was five years old. And we all laugh, comparing notes, knowing that we are all in this together despite our different timelines.

Then, suddenly, I crash, hit rock bottom—

I am in a darkened room, in a crib, clinging to the rail, looking through a doorway into the living room of my parents' first very small house in the new country, Canada, what we used to call fondly our *chandah*, or "shack." I am supposed to be asleep, but raised voices have excited me to wakefulness.

They are having a party. There are maybe half a dozen of them together, laughing, but mostly talking about the war, the chaotic music of their Polish words filling my darkness. Again, I am on the outside looking in; I watch them pass back and forth at the doorway, getting up for drinks and food. They are still young and vital at this time, I see.

I listen because they are telling stories, and I like stories. But these are war stories, not fairytales. That's what I was brought up on, I realize, now, in time present, war stories; I have never heard and do not actually know any Polish fairytales.

One "uncle" tells how he and my father got drunk one day and hijacked a flatbed truck loaded with bombs, for a joyride in the Italian countryside, to pick up vino. Crazy. They could have been killed, but, then, what did it matter? Look what happened at Monte Cassino: how out of their company of 220 men only 15 survived, and the slaughter went on day and night.

Now my mother talks, telling about one of her charges in the field hospital, how when she lifted the bloody sheets and saw that his limbs had been amputated—

And then she is with me, pulling me up out of the crib, stopping my cries. "Shhh. Be brave," she says. And then she brings me out of the darkness into the brightness of the party. And I see that everyone is in one piece, full of life, and they play with me.

The memory fades, and for a moment I am struck silent by its absence. My speech is abruptly finished; so I read congratulatory telegrams from the Premier of the province, the Leader of the Opposition, the Lieutenant Governor, and so on. Fifty years. Amazing. We all toast my parents, their friends offering best wishes, and the golden anniversary cake is brought out.

The party proceeds. After a while, my brother and I discover ourselves isolated on the edge of a conversation that has turned to more anguished Polish history, a heated argument about the Yalta agreement—how Poland was sacrificed to appease Russia. It is always like this, I realize: about the war, documenting the horrors, bearing witness.

After another *wodka*, my brother and I decide it is time to leave the old comrades to themselves, to their history. In the morning, I will fly back to the coast; tonight he and I can go out on our own, and talk about how some things never change.

At the door, heading into the frozen darkness, there are more hugs and kisses—and words. I bid my parents and my "aunts" and "uncles," each, in turn, *do widzenia*. The *solidarnosc* of surviving. That's what it's all about. Other riders, pale ones, may loiter in the wings, but I know I will never lose them—my family. Always I will have them, every time I speak, or think, in the words of my becoming.

Cover all the Mirrors...

One memento mori, stuffed in my bottom desk drawer along with funeral chapel memorabilia and some grainy black and white photographs, is a pamphlet entitled "At Home with Alzheimer's Disease," published, curiously enough, by CHMC Canada. On a trip back, I found it lying around unread in my parents' Winnipeg home, and numbly stuffed it into my suitcase. The dozen or so pages are full of helpful hints, like:

> *Do not wax floors—the slippery finish is treacherous and the shininess may create frightening reflections.*

Nothing, of course, in this handy publication addresses why; still, I flip through it in a talismanic way, hoping for clues. Everything about my father's fate remains a mystery. From my faraway west coast perspective, it seemed to just abruptly happen. But when I think about it, that's not exactly right; it's more complicated than that. Over many years of long-distance conversations and visits either way, my mother, no poster for mental health herself, had complained of oddities in his behaviour. He was cheap, miserly, silent, fussy; nothing so different from the twitchy marital discords I'd heard her lament for many years. But when anomalies started to add up, the doctors were summoned. After some back-and-forth, a diagnosis was developed—dementia—and then there was no going back. Rapidly, over the next two years, my father became increasingly unmanageable: to the point of madness.

But where, exactly, is that point? My mother decided to keep him home no matter what, because "he deserved it." As he disappeared—his mind, I mean—my father gradually lost his humanity, in a lugubriously tragic way. Some mysterious primal animal-self reared up and bit by bit assumed dominance. Eventually he became unrecognizable to us. Maybe even to himself.

Over those melancholy months, I came to visit, not as often as I could, but whenever guilt and family affection forced me. Living far away, I had the luxury of separation, of choice. Always on the plane, I'd try to imagine the worst, to bolster myself against surprise. It was always worse. Harrowing, of course, to see someone slip into the black hole of insanity while you stand by helpless. But in my case there was another element, another jolt; somehow my father's enigmatic symptoms (as is often the case, an absolute diagnosis was never limned) threw into sharp relief not only the inadequate framework by which we try to understand madness, but also a cryptic sense of my own father-son relationship.

> *Remove the bed frame so a fall out of bed will not be so damaging.*

I remember seeing my father after his first fall, his face the colour of bruised fruit. One eye was clouded from a broken blood vessel, his lips were scabbed from bites, his gaunt cheeks sprouted dead-white bristles, he had contusions on his hands, and the fingers on the right one hooked like a claw. His legs were wasted—one poised over the other like absurdly dainty crossbones. My father sat staring at me without recognition; or perhaps he was looking beyond me into a world of shadows populated with presences only he could perceive.

I could smell him across the room. He had always been a bit of a dandy, well turned out every day, in suit and tie mostly, even though in Canada he had never held a professional job. Now he sat quietly, still oddly dignified but a mockery of his former fastidious self. He wore a white shirt with blue pinstripes, buttoned at the neck and tucked neatly into Stanfield's long johns (safety-pinned at the waist to better hang on to his emaciated frame), a jaunty red beret on his bony head and ridiculous floppy slippers on his swollen feet. No tie. No pants. The shirt was stained and so were the long johns.

The family home was now a hospital, focused on the care of my father. At this early stage the doctors had tentatively concurred that the dementia manifested as Alzheimer's. The home care workers didn't care much about labels; to them treatability, not terminology was the issue. A rough humour informed their interactions with the patient. When he became troublesome and refused his usual mushy foods (mashed potatoes, Kraft Dinner, canned fruit, ice cream), they jollied him along, joking about "driving with Al." Naturally, they weren't torn up about his infantilization. Living with craziness demands many adjustments, I soon discovered; for one thing, you need a sense of irony, however crude, to buffer dread.

At first I tried to be rational. I told myself, it's not such a mystery. We all know something of madness, right? From literary and journalistic perspectives at least: Hamlet, Ophelia, Lear, Frankenstein (scientist, not monster), Phantom of the Opera, Kurtz, Hitler, Captain Queeg, Dr. Strangelove, not to mention the mundane range of psychos reported in the dailies. But none of that helps when you confront its actuality. For one thing, fictive and newsworthy lunacy is theatre, larger-than-life. Literary madfolk have vision, purpose, goals—often heroic, or at least they have a grandeur about them as they oppose the world in their determined execution of some one-pointed cause. The hoary notion that madmen see more—

and more clearly—than the normal person only adds to this glamour. Madness has always been associated with arcane wisdom: crazed seers, tranced shamen, fevered prophets, fanatical holy fools. Those who sunder themselves from the mundane through esoteric study or extraordinary circumstance acquire special status; they possess secret power, alternative knowledge, and maybe access to true reality.

Or maybe not. My father, as he sat in his modest living room, was none of the above. He never went out, did nothing in, said very little—merely smiled, laughed softly now and then, spit on the table, pissed on the rug, argued when anyone tried to help him. This seemed a domestic, everyday kind of madness with no redeeming dramatic features or wisdom attached. The banal household setting heightened, deepened the mystery; there was the kitchen, the TV, the mixmaster, the madman. Which one of these things "just doesn't belong"? Maybe they all do?

Was part of the problem that my father had been laid off too early, at fifty-seven, rather than retired at sixty-five like his friends? An old war injury had led to back problems; surgery made them worse. Lamed, retired, he had yet more time to do nothing at all. At first, he'd been anxious about survival without work and an income. But when his pensions kicked in, he relaxed. He became increasingly inwardly-focused, interacting with us less and less, only at dinner, rarely seeing friends, just sitting, staring out the window, sleeping during the day, limping up and down the stairs to the basement for no discernible reason at night, watching TV. Besides the nightly news, *Three's Company* became an inexplicable favourite, a show that seems rather rich in puns and double entendres for someone who didn't know English "so good." Maybe he just liked the girls.

When did it begin, exactly, I kept wondering, the inexorable pull away from this world to his own dark planet? My father had always been a little odd. Although he was gregarious at times in the company of those he liked, generally he was withdrawn, never sharing words or thoughts readily. The dominant image in my memory is of him in that living room, in the fading light, alone, not reading or doing, just being. We in the family had long before come to accept that as "normal," this solitary, detached individual, sitting on his own.

Looking back, I recalled a strange event at my parents' home: The Accident. This was a good fifteen years before we'd noticed any sign of madness. I'd driven in from the coast a few days earlier for a visit. Some of my friends had come by; I knew my father was bored, uncomfortable. So I asked him to move my car, just before four o'clock, when parking on the street expired for rush hour. He got up at once; this was the sort of task he liked, quiet, purposeful and solitary. And he was always interested in cars, not just driving them, but tinkering with the engines; after all, he had been a self-taught mechanic for many years.

It was a warm, luminous July afternoon, blindingly bright, the way it gets on the prairies. I remember my father going out the door in shirt sleeves, happy to escape. A few moments later we heard the sound of screeching tires, a thud, then a crash. We ran out. My Pontiac Le Mans was a wreck, its front accordioned into the rear end of a parked truck, its own rear-end chrome twisted and torn, the trunk squashed. Then my father stumbled up the steps, blood from a deep gash on his forehead dripping down like red tears on his white shirt. With the help of witnesses, we pieced it together: He'd gotten in, reversed wildly up onto the sidewalk a hundred metres, knocking down a phone booth, and narrowly missing two pedestrians. Then the car lurched forward, going fast, got down off the sidewalk and plowed into a parked truck

"What happened?" we asked him. But we never found out. My father said only that the car had "gone crazy" and never spoke of the incident again. His dignity would not bear it.

> *Move furniture from the centre of rooms...to allow for pacing and circular wandering.*

By the second visit, post-diagnosis, my father had stopped watching Suzanne Somers; he spent all his time roaming the house. When I found him in his favourite spot in the living room, for the moment at rest, I sat down with him.

He grinned, then muttered: "Those shoes; my, my, those shoes." I asked: "What shoes, what about them?" Were these shoes out of his childhood, a numinous image from the past that might tell me something about the mysterious reorientation going on in his head? Or some other kind? Bronzed baby shoes, red Oz shoes, golden princess slippers, "the-time-has-come-to-talk-of-many-things" shoes? Or just my runners, catching his errant eye? I needed details to help piece the puzzle together.

"*Tell* me about the shoes," I urged. He shook his head, sadly, as if acknowledging the gulf between us, perhaps the futility of our attempts at communication, present and past. *This* madness seemed more philosophical, but maybe only to someone clutching for meaning. As if to underscore my confusion, my father laughed abruptly—an empty mechanical hacking sound.

He was smaller than I remembered, under 40 kilos, as if shrinking into his clothes, sinking into the chesterfield, more withered homunculus than the flesh-and-blood father who had towered over me and ruled from a distance my childhood world. A poseur, a midget impostor was before me—a trickster bodying forth a satiric sketch of what "father" has meant to me over the years. He wavered through a spectrum of familiar attributes: authority figure, provider, WWII soldier, immigrant worker, survivor, and, finally, hopeless victim in a battle against chaos.

But hadn't he always been like that, unknowable, an enigma? When I'd moved to the coast, for instance, he did not visit, call, or write. He had never interacted much with me. All through grade school I'd heard about father-son stuff, activities you did together, but fun things, not like going to church on Good Friday or to the hardware store for nails. By grade six I became obsessed with this idea, that my father and I should actually go out and *do something,* just the two of us, like those legendary sons and dads.

After much intervention by my mother, it was decided we'd go to the Starland Theatre on Main Street one Saturday night. My father never did anything North American like going to movies, so this was special. My memory of the film is vague—I was overexcited, I guess. It was a black and white thriller, the characters trapped in a fatal, monochromatic reality. I don't recall much except one scene in which a starved escaped convict breaks into an isolated cabin and wolfs down most of a loaf of sliced white bread. For some reason, that image locked in my mind. My father hardly said a word through the evening. As soon as the credits began, we marched home in silence and he went straight to bed. We never did anything "fun" again.

He always was elusive—when I was growing up, when I became an adult, and, then, when he turned into a child in his madness, moving relentlessly further and further away from me, from all of us. I'd learned to respect that autonomy as an adult; we were, after all, separate people with separate lives. But it was a poignant breakthrough to understand that now, as he descended into Alzheimer's, there was no longer any way of bridging such gaps, even symbolically.

My father still knew me as his son. No final diagnosis had been reached; my mother just kept repeating, "He's not himself, he's strange." But my father had always been strange and a stranger. Perhaps the strangest part was that at this stage, when he was first being tipped into official madness, we talked (in Polish) as never before, son and father, I mean. In a companionate way, sitting together in the dimming, curtained living room. He was still aware of the outside world beyond the sheltering walls of home, the larger frame of reference we both inhabited.

Politics had always been important at home. Now, we agreed, so much had happened. The collapse of the Berlin Wall, of Communism itself, all that. The old Europe of my father's pre-immigrant life was gone; he'd never traveled back to see the new order emerging, and, in a way, I suspect, did not really believe that Communism was dismantled. When we watched TV news briefly, he scoffed at any assertion that things could *really* change. "How can anyone understand what is happening anymore?" he asked, shaking his head. It was all "crazy shit."

Maybe *that's* what madness is, in one embodiment: an inability to go along with change, a hankering to hold on to the known and familiar, to resist and perforce be broken on the wheel of inevitability? Some people just aren't very adaptable. I remember the story of an elderly aunt who would not believe that men actually landed on the moon, that they hopped and skipped like kids on its powdery grey surface. I'd laughed, then.

Or maybe madness has more to do with personality itself, the intangible factors of our separately individuated selves. There was always a stubborn streak in my father, a core of stolid peasant obstinacy, distrust, and scepticism in the face of the new and different. That which was known was known, claimed as refuge; everything else was absurd—more "crazy shit." Once, when I came for a visit and had my notebook computer with me, he laughed when I tried to show him how it worked, refused to even look—as if claiming to have a portable computer was the most ludicrous proposition imaginable. Another time I brought a videotape I'd made of our neighbourhood to show him where I lived, how different it was in Vancouver. Images of our house, my partner, me, the church at the corner. I rented a VCR, plugged it in, ran the video; he turned his back on the TV and stared out the window instead.

Was my father's madness, then, partly self-generated, an elaborate game of disbelief he played with himself, a wilful way of denying a baffling world? I want to think there's a measure of will to it, that one must participate in one's madness—that there's more to it than chemical imbalances, diet, or using aluminum pots for cooking.

> *Distract the AD person from escaping through windows or doors by camouflaging them with decorations...*

By my third visit, I had become divided in my father's mind, part of his new binary system of thought. This seemed the demarcation line. For a while you can be both mad and sane, sliding between these poles. Then the inevitable happens; eventually one loses control over the evolution of one's madness.

This formulation for some reason appeals to me; it seems to make sense. At least, that's what I told myself then.

The house was now my father's exclusive domain. The Known—inside—was manageable, safe. Beyond this lay the Unknown, a realm of strangers—menacing, impinging outside reality that he could do nothing about. In the Known, my father spent his days and nights fine-tuning controls: endlessly fiddling with locks, handles, switches, knobs; rearranging the contents of his dresser drawers, closets, pockets; closing, locking, opening, and re-closing doors and windows. He passed many hours nailing furniture to walls and floors, screwing drawers down to keep them shut, and so on. Though familiar and contained, every square inch of the Known needed constant scrutiny—as if the thingness of it were in danger of flying off into space.

Perhaps to throw off potential enemies, he became unpredictable. His patterns of eating and sleeping dissolved and reformed. He refused favourite foods, ate with gusto that which he had spurned as garbage in the old days: pizza, hot dogs. Sleeping and waking turned upside down, too. Sometimes he stayed in bed for eighteen hours, then roamed from midnight to dawn, muttering, lurching from room to room, cursing, dismantling appliances to make sure they were operating correctly.

Though weak and crippled, he was now full of nasty energy, hitting my mother, spitting out pills, abusing the care workers, deliberately knocking over drinks and plates of food, shredding his bedding into maddeningly straight strips of cloth, trying to set the house on fire with bits of paper under the stove elements. He'd always been a gentle man, yet I'm sure that in the grip of this derangement he would have killed his wife of almost sixty years, if only he'd had the strength. He no longer trusted anyone and believed he did not need her for anything. Though actually helpless, he thought himself entirely his own master—and could not tolerate interference with his will. And it seemed that any outside being was that, an unwarranted interference with his absolute will. There was no longer room for her, for anyone, in his newly streamlined universe.

My father's domain was compromised, of course, despite his constant vigilance. Intruders kept getting in, like me, or rather different semblances of me. At some late period in the dementia, I became two people to him: me, the oldest son (familiar, safe), and the other me, the "mysterious guest" (enigmatic, threatening, interesting), who was staying upstairs in the spare room. We played an elaborate game of Hide and Seek. I'd spot him peeking around a doorway, watching "me," that latter me, the interloper. Shaving in the morning, I might catch him in my mirror. He kept on the lookout, monitoring the movements of the two "me"s. How confounding to see me, the son, and then—in the blink of an eye—that enigmatic other, the mysterious unwanted guest who had come out of nowhere and wouldn't go away.

When I'd encounter him, he'd grin, not like his old self, but a new, boyish creature, a kid playing charades whose secret is suddenly found out. "Peek-a-boo, I see you," I'd say, in English. We'd laugh, though I'm pretty sure he did not understand. Back and forth we flip-flopped, the three of us—him, me, the mysterious stranger. Now, at last, we were playing: the question of identity itself had become a game.

At other times I'd sit with him and we'd talk, all three of us, getting along quite well. Then he'd turn to me, uneasy: "What do you think he [me the "stranger," that is] wants here?" He addressed me informally, his son, the Known; then suddenly he would switch, as I metamorphosed into the object of our attention, to elevated diction, using the formal Polish *pan* for "sir," his sentences taking on a more mannered tone. "And so, sir, are you having an enjoyable journey?" What did it mean that *that* was me, this "gentleman," a more distinguished and important aspect of myself, in my father's sliding mind? Maybe just that I was, always had been, a stranger.

> *Cover all the mirrors in the house and keep curtains drawn at night. Reflections can be very frightening to people with dementia when they do not recognize the people in the reflections.*

The final visit was starker, down to basics. Familial connections were severed by the radical simplification of disease; my father no longer knew me at all. When I arrived, my mother reminded him: "Frank, it's your son." He looked up at me from the bed and smiled slyly, pretending to go along. But I sensed he knew it was just another trick, that I was one of the caregivers, hoping to get at his money, maybe—the treasure trove. He grinned, that disturbing alien twinkle in his eye, and said: "Peek-a-boo."

The money: for an uncertain period, perhaps even prior to the onset of the disease, my father had tried to save himself with dollars, cramming pickle jars with $100 and $50 bills from his monthly pension cheques. About a dozen jars were eventually discovered in his bedroom closet, yielding over $34,000. The money kept him busy. He spent many long evenings tallying the cash with his bedroom door shut, rummaging in the closet, refusing to let anyone in. When his control finally slipped, he lost track of the money, where it was, what it meant.

Control was a major theme of my father's insanity. His mad dominion kept shrinking, from the world at large, to his house, to the main floor, to, finally, his stripped-down bare-essentials bedroom with its double bed, one bureau, two windows with see-through curtains, a couple of pillows, a coverlet. He took then to marking his territory. After a painter came one afternoon to redo his room in exactly the same beige it had always been, my father meticulously pissed on each of the newly painted walls.

As the final failing weeks dragged on, he slipped into a deeper and darker primitivism, a primal state where nothing much matters because you are truly free, like a very young child, to spit, piss, shit, anywhere, anytime. At the end, my father achieved a fundamental if inhuman freedom of the self; he died untrammeled by consciousness, not knowing what was happening to him. Neither did we; a minor infection had gone unnoticed by the caregivers and now needed hospital treatment. On the ward he deteriorated rapidly; three days, and he was gone, at age seventy-seven.

I wondered, though, if my father had been moving toward this mad terminus for many more years than encompassed by the actual Alzheimer's. Long after the funeral, back home on the coast, I continued to pursue this new interest, reading of the now famous Nun Study related to dementia, how those traced over decades in the convent revealed, or not, the disease according to their levels of language ability: the less expressive the writing style, the more chance of early senility and worse. Communicating clearly and effectively was not enough, according to the data. Only writing that was vivid, lively, and imaginative, proved in the long run to be predictive of sustained mental hygiene. Later I came across another study, of Japanese retirees in Hawaii, which claimed that those who lived in a linguistic ghetto, i.e., speaking their own rather than learning the language of the land, were more prone to early Alzheimer's.

Both my parents, especially my father, lived out their Canadian life in an immigrant enclave, in Winnipeg's ethnic North End, learning just enough English to get by in their low-end jobs, not entering into the culture in any way—speaking Polish to their Polish friends, going to a Polish church, and so on, while, of course, being actually cut off from the true richness and complexity of that socio-linguistic matrix. My father never found anything meaningful in the new world to talk about in its language. He derided its incomprehensible manifestations, the technology, infotainment, youth culture, everything. He did not engage, but rather stood apart. Perhaps that very detachment and denial are what made those issues of chaos/control so insurmountable when they surfaced in the illness.

Could it be, then, that madness is embedded not just in our genes or utensils but in our very words, the language we use, or don't use, every day? That our words may well be the counters of our existence, the markers of our souls? Does that, perhaps, make us, finally, responsible for our own sanity? To me, at least, this is an attractive theory, though its appeal makes it suspect. Will words save me? Can reality be nailed down, as my father had hoped, but with language, not hammers and nails? If so, I could add a tip to that handy CMHC handbook:

> *Read deeply, be loquacious, write colourfully, spiritedly, even floridly...*

Or not. The last time I saw my father was at the Cropo Chapel on Main Street, on the evening of prayers, his body restored by funereal arts to an eerie imitation of his former pre-mad self: hair cut and combed, cheeks shaved, nails trimmed and cleaned, face in seeming repose—instead of the crazed, vacant creature he had become near the end.

After everyone was gone, I took some photos of my father, iconic images for my mother to send back to the Old Country. I got up close. The ends of his fingers looked waxy, the nails an icy pink. His eyelids thinned to translucent films of flesh; his ears glowed luminous white; a shiny whiteness emanated from his brow. I bent closer to his face, to search for my reflection.

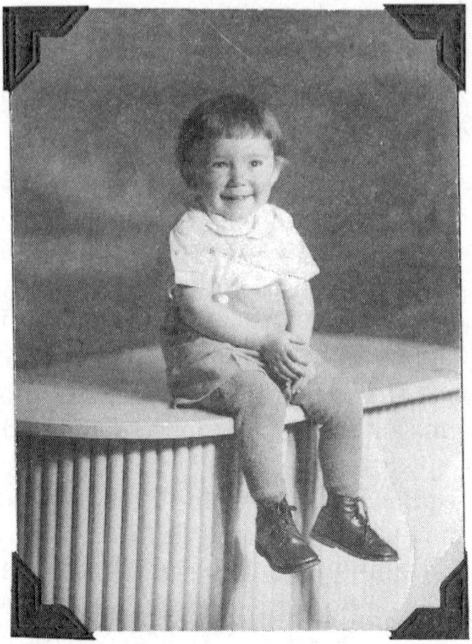

POSTSCRIPT: TIME-TRIPPING

Every time I go back to Winnipeg, my visit starts with the same sentimental journey, covering strange yet familiar ground, getting my bearings on the quirky terrain of memory.

From the airport, it's a fairly straightforward drive. Passing through the old city core, heading northward, streets and avenues expose vistas of urban desolation. Churches stand empty, for sale. Many houses and former businesses are boarded up; others have disappeared, bulldozed down, their lots paved over, leaving a streetscape of apparent parking lots—except that there are no cars. Just big blanks. I start to get a spacey, surreal feeling driving along, as if the city had been bombed, or suffered some other catastrophe long ago, and had never been rebuilt, just the rubble removed.

Then I'm zooming down the easy slope of Salter Bridge, past the monolithic Winnipeg Cold Storage, which squats like a giant bunker on the left, to see the big sign on Dufferin Street, high atop an auto repair shop: "Welcome to the North End"—my destination, dead ahead.

But it's not the same. For Sale signs and empty houses abound in my old neighbourhood. Selkirk Avenue—the main drag from a pan-Slavic perspective way back when—is depressed, distressed, and generally disenfranchised, a grotty, ever less perambulated version of downtown Main Street, with even more blank and boarded-up storefronts. Everyone is getting the hell out of the good old North End. Why? The outlying districts, where second and third immigrant generations have established themselves, are, to my nostalgic eyes, bland, sprawls of ugly though no doubt comfortable housing, dull empty streets, and tacky stop'n'grab strip malls. Ironically enough, Winnipeg still hosts Folklorama every summer, a week-long indulgence of all that is vibrantly diverse in Canadian society, and the venues nowadays are mostly in the North End, that is, in a locale increasingly devoid of the thriving ethnicity that gave rise to the original hoopla.

So it goes—and I go, driving on through the different strata of my youth: passing the churches and schools I attended; North End houses we lived in, or rather the spots where those homes, one really just a shack, once stood; community halls I was taken to on snowy nights for weddings, with me sitting the feet of the polka band's drummer, fascinated by the rhythms of the skins, bringing him drinks from the bar every half hour; stores I ran errands to, under different, mostly Euro names back then; pine-paneled basement rec rooms, where I hung out with buddies, drank and smoked joints until we all got red-eyed and weirdly hungry; parks where I first kissed girls in the dark; places that used to be alluring shadowy pool halls, smoky, quiet, meditative, now neon-bright, muzak-blaring Shoppers Drug Marts.

Eventually, I'll reach the Holy Ghost Cemetery on the highway to Lockport and other points north, to visit my father's grave, and the graves of friends of the family. Windswept, barren, especially in winter, it seems the right place for my dad, a gentle man who remained in what seemed a lonely psychic space all the years I knew him. Then I'll console myself with a bite at Kelekis for old times' sake, as I do once a trip, always ordering the same things, food I never have anywhere else: a hot dog with shoestring fries and coleslaw. Though it's in a different location than when I started going there, with luck, the same Kelekis sisters that have been running the place since my high school days will be behind the counter, looking much the same, doling out food and good cheer as usual.

After that, I'll circle back westward toward my brother's cozy, vaguely hobbit-like home in the West End. We'll sit and talk over drinks. I'll watch him smoke, suddenly think about something long-forgotten: like how I dropped him on his head when he was a baby, in his pram, me taking him out for a ride, going down too hard off a tall curb, and, terrified, never told anyone. He *seems* OK now. If things are relaxed, maybe I'll even share with him my latest nuggets of Peg trivia, like this fascinating factoid that, according to Maple Leaf Foods Incorporated, the residents of the province of Manitoba, land of so many fine smoked meats, consumes *seven times* the national average of Klik, Canada's Spam clone, the pink pressed-pork that WWII Canadian vets were exposed to overseas and strangely, disturbingly, craved on their return.

Then I'll be ready to visit our mother, old now and crazy in a different way, her ceaseless, scary energy and indomitable will finally pushed under by years and meds, living in care at Deer Lodge Hospital—where she apparently thinks her sons are Prince Harry and the other one, those so-called noble heirs to the British throne. Go figure. Or maybe she'll think I'm her brother, long-dead, or even an uncle from her girlhood in Poland. Apparently I resemble both, more and more as I get older, in her sliding mind, especially when I wear a hat. Must remember not to wear one. I am a bad son, increasingly dreading these realities, evading duty while fearing the time that duty will disappear: denial. Partly, I suppose, I want to retain the mother in my head, who knew me at least, who let me stay out all night as long as I was up for early morning mass next day, who called me Bolshevik with her special blend of scorn and irritated affection.

In such ways the trip will pass, shuffling between family connections and solitude, the booze flowing—thinking about the ethnic crucible where I grew up—the North End very much alive in my head. Then it's back on the plane. As the flight attendant makes her runic gestures, I look around at my fellow passengers: some Chinese, some turbaned, a few Africans—the usual mix heading for what must be Canada's most multicultural city—even maybe a few like me, secret ethnics, invisible ones. The thought takes me back to something, a call for submissions to a proposed TV series called something like *13 Stories About Love*. I was interested, had a story to tell, I thought, a bittersweet tale of love and culture...but when I reached the section on creative team, it stipulated at least one applying member must be "diverse," and glossed the term this way:

> Visible minority (including but not limited to, Aboriginal (Status, Non-Status, Metis or Inuit), or members of visible minority group: persons who are non-Caucasian in race or non-white in colour. Please note that visible minority is determined by race or colour, not by place of birth or nationality. Members of visible minorities in Canada include: Black (e.g. African, Haitian, Jamaican, Somali), Chinese, South Asian (e.g. Punjabi, Sri Lankan, Bangladeshi, Pakistani), Arab/West Asian (e.g. Armenian, Egyptian, Iranian, Lebanese, Moroccan), Filipino, South East Asian (e.g. Cambodian, Indonesian, Laotian, Vietnamese), Latin American, Japanese, Korean, and any other non-white racial group not identified) or member of other minority group (including but not limited to gay/lesbian men women, or the physically or mentally challenged).

And my long-standing Polish-Canadian identity was no more. Cut adrift on the sea of diversity, my pale face bobbing there like some soggy piece of white bread, I was troubled—bugged, even—by this new truth. Now, looking around again at the faces of my fellow passengers on the plane, my tired post-visit mind drifts, playing with the notion of measurable ethnicity, of testing each traveler, giving each of us a number, a grade or percentage, and I find myself imagining a new consumer product, an ethnic testing kit neatly packaged in one of those impregnable plastic bubbles, adorned with little red maple leaves here and there. I can almost hear the TV ad: "available *only* at Canadian Tire; add the bodily fluid of your choice to discover your absolute cultural currency, whenever diversity drift or ethnic ennui occurs." And then their theme song, "I'll start with you," is it? But start with whom? Who am I, if not ethnic?

Suddenly a gentle tap on the shoulder brings me back to reality. The flight attendant, pretty, with a slight, unidentifiable accent, wants to offer me something. A soft drink? A glass of wine? A fluid of some kind. She is drawing me away from questions of cultural authenticity, pulling me into the immediate, shared experience of traveling back to Vancouver, away from Winnipeg, from my experience of Polish-Canadian hyphenation, of difference. I'm a little hung over, in that after-family-visiting sort of way, but I ask for a glass of white wine, Canadian, of course, and she smiles.

ACKNOWLEDGMENTS

Deepest thanks to Michèle Adams, a gifted writer and editor who generously and energetically took time from her own projects to work on this collection, offering inspiration, direction, and many proof marks.

My gratitude as well to the University College of the Fraser Valley for supporting the development of the book at several key points.

And, of course, thank you to family and friends I grew up with. That was mostly in the 1960s and 70s, the time of Expo and Pierre Elliott Trudeau, an elegant enigma in his swirling cloak and red rose boutonnière. Folk dances in community centres, ethnic food fairs, exotic costumes, celebrations of origins: colourful carnivals of diversity athrob throughout the land. That was us way back then, when an enraptured Canada discovered its multicultural soul. One community reflected this new vision as if in a cunningly handcrafted mirror—Winnipeg's polyglot North End, a neighbourhood where immigrants from different (though at that time almost exclusively European) origins lived side by side in hard-working harmony—the spitting image of wholeness through diversity. At least sometimes. Welcome to my special neighbourhood.

P.S. To dentists everywhere: keep up the good work.

Photos